FEASTING
on
HERBS

Sue Lawrence

FEASTING
on HERBS

with photographs by Victor Albrow

KYLE CATHIE LIMITED

First published in paperback in Great Britain 1997 by
Kyle Cathie Limited
20 Vauxhall Bridge Road, London SW1V 2SA

ISBN 1 85626 233 2

A Cataloguing in Publication record for this title is available from the British Library

Design by Lisa Steffens
Typed by Rollo Book Services Limited
Typeset by Heronwood Press
Printed by Butler & Tanner Ltd, Frome, Somerset

The publishers wish to thank Thomas Goode & Co. (London) Ltd., Jenners of Edinburgh,
Gillian Cathie and Wedgewood for the loan of props used in the photographs; Scotherbs
and Valvona and Crolla for ingredients; and Jackie Haddon for recipe tasting.

contents

This book is dedicated to Robert Wilson of Scotherbs
for all his help

introduction

Feast on herbs; they are worth it! Fresh herbs add flavour, colour, texture and vitality to any dish. Now they are readily available in packets from supermarkets, delicatessens and even from your local corner shop. They can be bought potted up to sit on a sunny windowsill; you can buy packets of seed to plant in the garden; but however you buy them, use herbs in abundance.

I have selected twenty of my favourites from the vast list of herbs on offer. I want to show how versatile they are and how they need not be restricted to so-called classical combinations such as lamb with mint or salmon with dill. By trial and error you can discover which flavours work together. If you have neither time nor inclination to experiment yourself, then take my word for it and try the combinations in my recipes!

As a general rule, the more pungent and assertive flavours usually work better with equally dominant flavours. The traditional marriage of game with thyme, both very British, can be altered to use a herb more recently imported from, say, Europe or the Far East. Try venison with marjoram; cook rabbit with coriander or basil. Fish has endless possibilities which stretch far beyond the ubiquitous parsley sprig used to garnish the Dover sole. Shellfish and smoked fish can often blend with strong flavours; try mussels with oregano or scallops with sweet cicely. Use smoked mackerel with sage or fennel; smoked haddock with lovage or flat-leaf parsley. 'Meaty' fish such as fresh tuna works very well with punchy chives, celery-flavoured lovage or even that archetypal lamb accompaniment, mint.

Vegetables, cheese and egg dishes work with most herbs, and indeed, simple – even bland – dishes such as scrambled eggs or omelettes, can be elevated to gourmet status by the addition of some freshly chopped herbs such as chervil, rocket, sorrel or tarragon. Mashed potatoes become a meal in themselves by stirring in basil or rocket pesto just before serving. A quick 3 minute omelette is made into an appetising feast by the addition of finely chopped tarragon, savory or chervil. By chopping some sage, oregano or chives into macaroni cheese, you can convert a nursery food into a gastronomic delight.

Thus herbs play an intrinsic role both as enhancer of otherwise ordinary dishes and as flavouring. With subtle flavoured ingredients, the addition of herbs will really sing out loud and clear. Add them with discretion for fear of overpowering everything else.

Herbs can be the main ingredient, too. Produce a whole new taste sensation by making luscious bay ice-cream. Or make a herb salad with both leaves and flowers tossed into well-dressed salad leaves. Make a pesto sauce with coriander, mint, parsley or rosemary as a change from basil. Make sharp, refreshing sorrel into a vibrant green soup.

At barbecue time, tie bunches of the more robust herbs such as rosemary and thyme and dip into olive oil or a marinade, then use instead of a pastry brush to baste grilled meat or fish. Strip long, woody stems of herbs such as sage or rosemary and use the stems as kebab sticks instead of metal skewers. You can also use herb oils made from a variety of strongly-flavoured herbs; bay, basil, thyme and tarragon are ideal. These can be brushed onto grilled or barbecued foods, used to fry or roast vegetables, fish and meats, brushed over freshly-made breads and drizzled over pizzas. Herb vinegars, made commonly from tarragon, basil, marjoram, thyme and mint, also work well to dress salads. They make very welcome gifts, too.

Think of colour and texture. That most herbs are green is rather an obvious statement, but there are many shades of green. And, of course, most of them change colour during cooking, invariably becoming darker and sometimes duller. You often find, therefore, that recipes stipulate the addition of freshly chopped herbs at the end of the cooking, so as to preserve the freshness of the colour. Texture is also important: rosemary should always be chopped very finely, or kept whole and removed at the end of the cooking. Soft leaves such as tarragon and coriander can be chopped less vigorously, for their fine texture means they merge in easily with the other ingredients.

The freshness of herbs is of paramount importance. You can keep herbs, as I do, in large terracotta pots if garden space is at a premium. Basil, chives, coriander, marjoram, oregano, parsley, rosemary, sage and thyme can all be grown on a windowsill. Best of all is to pick or cut from your own garden or pot just when you are about to use them in the recipe. This is not always possible or practical. But everywhere today there are herb-growers supplying the freshest of herbs to many outlets. My supplier here in Scotland imports many out-of-season herbs during the winter months and so is able to supply a huge variety throughout the whole year. Then there are supermarket packets which are a marvellous standby, although often in meagre sized bags and expensive too.

Keep herbs in a cool place or in the salad drawer of the refrigerator. Some, such as sorrel and basil, do better kept out of the fridge, but somewhere dark. Place herbs from the garden in a glass of water if you are to use them within an hour or so. Otherwise place them in a large, sealed polythene bag in the refrigerator. Only wash herbs if absolutely essential, for example if you are not sure they are scrupulously clean, or if there is danger of chemical sprays having been used. Herbs are less robust than salad leaves and need to be dried carefully.

For chopping large amounts of herbs, I like to use a semi-lunar knife. Some cooks swear by a mouli herb chopper. The flavour of most herbs becomes stronger if the leaves are 'bruised' slightly by rubbing between your fingers, rather than brutally treated. The metal blade of the food processor, however, seems to have no adverse effects on the basil in pesto. Although many food writers are adamant that herbs should always be torn or shredded, never chopped, I confess I tear and shred them with my fingers primarily to have the glorious aroma on my fingers!

In all the recipes, measurements of herbs are for whole leaves before chopping. Always measure out your whole herb leaves first (stripped of stems or stalks if necessary). Then chop or shred as required. Eggs are always medium (size 3), unless otherwise stated. All teaspoons and tablespoons are level, not heaped, unless stated. Finally, although all recipes give quantities in both metric and imperial units, follow only one or the other and never mix the two!

Once you have followed these uncomplicated recipes and experimented yourself, you will discover how pleasurable cooking with herbs can be. They provide colour, flavour and texture. They are healthy and invigorating; add them with zest and gusto. You need only add a couple of leaves to a dish to transform an ordinary meal into a memorable feast, proof enough of their inestimable value.

Sue Lawrence
December 1994

chapter 1

basil

In this country, there are two main types of basil: the one we know and love, sweet basil (*Ocimum basilicum*) and bush basil (*Ocimum minimum*). The latter is a small plant, only growing to about 6 inches high. There is also a popular hybrid form, opal (or purple) basil, whose leaves are dark purple, almost bronze in colour. Although the bush and opal basils have a very similar taste to sweet basil, the flavours are thought to be inferior. They are both, however, useful for their decorative qualities. The purple coloured basil leaves, for example, are wonderful shredded into salads, or kept whole, as a garnish, where sweet basil has been used in the actual cooking.

Sweet basil is a rather delicate annual herb, which cannot withstand the merest hint of frost. That is why I would advise that you keep a couple of pots of basil on your kitchen window-ledge, to pluck off leaves at will. If you are lucky enough to live in a frost-free zone, then sow basil seeds in a sunny sheltered position, preferably in a light, rich soil. You can lift plants from the ground before the onset of the winter frosts, and grow them as pot plants either on that sunny window-sill or in a greenhouse.

It is believed that basil came from India. The flavour and smell of basil simply exudes sunshine. Whether this is because so many of us have first encountered basil in some sunny Mediterranean country, or whether the aromatic smell is reminiscent of food usually associated with hotter countries, it matters not. Having been drawn by the alluring, sweet smell, it is then the taste, slightly peppery, with a hint of cloves, which turns normally sane adults into basil addicts at first bite.

Although dried basil is available, it is not worth even trying. If you do happen to have a glut of fresh basil, then you can preserve it for use during the winter months. My favourite method is to make lots of fresh pesto (see page 3) and freeze it in individual pots. Or it can be kept for up to 6 weeks in a screw-top jar in the fridge. Otherwise, preserve it in oil; pack the dry leaves into a wide-necked jar, layering with salt as you go, then top up with olive oil and seal tightly. You can also make basil vinegar by the same method as I give later for tarragon vinegar (see page 160). Try to avoid chopping the delicate leaves, unless you have to as they turn black very easily: they respond better to being shredded with the fingers. Since basil is now most at home in those countries surrounding the Mediterranean, use it with ingredients usually associated with their style of cooking: tomatoes, courgettes, aubergines, pasta, salads, and also with poultry, fish and eggs.

I like to toss it into soups, stews or pasta dishes, at the very end of cooking. In fact, I tend to toss it into almost everything: that is the sign of true addiction!

Tomato Summer Pudding

This is summer pudding with a difference! Although it is made with bread and fruit – the usual components – the bread is Marmite-smeared toast and the fruit is tomatoes. The idea is a continuation of a favourite breakfast dish in my family: Marmite on toast, with grilled tomatoes. The Italian idea of serving toast, rubbed with garlic and a cut tomato (bruschetta) also came into play. So what has resulted is a rather unusual, but quite delicious loaf-shaped summer pudding, which can be served either as a starter or, if you cut down on the garlic, as a breakfast dish. Although you can use white bread, I prefer the savoury, almost nutty, overtones of good wholemeal bread. Depending on how much you like Marmite (Vegemite would be a good substitute), spread it thickly or thinly. It is important to drain the tomatoes very well indeed, over a sieve, until they are almost dry, otherwise the pudding will be too liquid to stand up, once decanted. Also, be sure to season very generously: lots of salt and pepper and some sugar too, to bring out the flavour of the tomatoes. Try to use tomatoes which have ripened under the sun, for their flavour is superior to the bland, insipid, watery tomatoes on offer in the winter months. (serves 4)

6–7 slices of wholemeal bread, crusts removed
Marmite
butter for greasing
2 tablespoons olive oil
3 garlic cloves, peeled and finely chopped
2¼–2½ lb/1.05–1.1 kg tomatoes, skinned
salt, pepper
1 teaspoon sugar
8–10 large basil leaves

---

1. Toast the bread lightly on one side, using a grill, rather than a toaster. Spread the untoasted sides with Marmite.

2. Lightly butter a 1 lb/500 g loaf tin. With the Marmite sides facing in, use the bread to line the base and sides, making sure there are no gaps, patching them up with pieces of bread.

3. Heat the oil, and fry the garlic and tomatoes gently for about 5 minutes. Season generously with salt, pepper and sugar. Then drain very well over a sieve.

4. Using a slotted spoon, spoon half the tomatoes into the breadcase. Place the whole basil leaves over the top. Season again, then top with the remaining tomatoes. Press down as much as you can. (You might not be able to get all the tomatoes in, but do press down well.)

5. Top with the remaining bread slices, toast-side up. Cover with clingfilm, then place on a plate. Put a suitable weight on top (I usually use a tin, plus several small weights from my kitchen scales) and place in the fridge over night.

6. Next day, remove the weights and clingfilm, loosen the edges with a knife, then decant carefully on to a plate. Cut into thick slices and serve at room temperature.

NOTE: Do not freeze.

Tomato and Mozzarella Salad

For this most simple of salads, it is important to have best quality ingredients. First of all, ensure that the tomatoes actually taste of something. For the cheese, do try to buy real Italian buffalo Mozzarella. The soft texture of the 'real thing' is also vastly superior to the rubbery look-alikes. The sun-dried tomatoes should be preserved in extra-virgin olive oil, for you will be using some of the oil from the jar as a salad dressing. Finally, pick the largest, most beautiful basil leaves for this extremely colourful and tasty salad. It should be served with plenty of Italian bread, such as ciabatta or focaccia. (serves 4)

> 3 large tomatoes
> 8 oz/250 g Italian Mozzarella, sliced
> 12–16 large basil leaves
> 2 tablespoons sun-dried tomatoes (preserved in oil), drained from
>   their oil and slivered
> 1 tablespoon olive oil from the jar of tomatoes
> 2 tablespoons extra-virgin olive oil
> salt, pepper

Slice the tomatoes fairly thickly and arrange them in rows, on a large flat serving plate, overlapping with the slices of Mozzarella. Tuck the basil leaves in between the slices at regular intervals, then sprinkle over the sun-dried tomatoes. Drizzle over the oil from the jar, then the 2 tablespoons olive oil. Season well with freshly milled salt and pepper. Serve with plenty of warmed, fresh Italian bread. NOTE: Do not freeze.

Pesto

Pesto sauce arrived from Liguria in northern Italy in the late 1980s, and has reigned supreme ever since. The traditional ingredients were basil, pine kernels and Parmesan. Now there are pestos made from coriander, parsley, mint or rosemary. Pecans, walnuts or macadamias are often used in place of pine kernels. And the cheese can be anything from Parmesan to Pecorino – any hard, strongly-flavoured cheese. The classic use of pesto, and possibly still the best, is to toss a good spoonful into freshly cooked pasta and garnish with shavings of Parmesan, toasted pine kernels or sprigs of basil, but pesto is an unbelievably versatile sauce. Try adding a teaspoonful to vinaigrette, or to egg custard for savoury tarts. Put it on baked potatoes, in garlic bread mix, in thick, American club, or Italian picnic-loaf sandwiches. A dollop in vegetable, tomato or fish soups adds flavour. Or make a crust for grilled fish or meat by mixing it with breadcrumbs. Pesto can be stored in a screw-top jar in the fridge for up to 6 weeks, or in the freezer for several months. (makes enough to fill 1 lb/500 g jar)

> 2½ oz/65 g basil leaves
> 2 garlic cloves, peeled and crushed
> 2 oz/50 g Parmesan, freshly grated
> 2 oz/50 g pine kernels, toasted for 2–3 minutes (take care, they burn quickly!)
> ¼ teaspoon salt
> about 4 fl oz/125 ml extra-virgin olive oil

Place the first 5 ingredients in a food processor and process until combined. Then, with machine running, slowly add sufficient oil to provide a thick paste. Taste for seasoning.

Pesto and Goat's Cheese Pizza

This is a pizza with a difference. Since basil and tomatoes go so well together, the tomato-covered base is spread with a thick layer of fresh pesto sauce, then scattered with basil leaves just before baking. The basil leaves can be either the green or the purple ones. They become wonderfully crunchy and crisp when baked in the hot oven. The cheese is not the usual pizza cheese, Mozzarella, but a more powerful goat's cheese, which melts equally well in the oven. Try to buy a goat's cheese which is neither too young and fresh, nor too mature and 'goaty'. This is a very easy dish to prepare, the only important thing to remember is to start at least 1½–2 hours in advance to allow time for the dough to rise. Serve it hot with a simple green salad. (serves 2–3)

<u>Base</u>
10 oz/300 g strong white flour, sifted
1 teaspoon easy-blend dried yeast
¼ teaspoon salt
1 tablespoon olive oil
5 fl oz/150 ml tepid water (hand-hot)

<u>Topping</u>
2 tablespoons tomato purée
2 heaped tablespoons pesto
6 oz/175 g goat's cheese, rind removed and diced
   (weight after removing rind)
1 tablespoon olive oil
8–10 basil leaves (green or purple)

1. Combine the flour, yeast and salt in a bowl. Then add the oil, and sufficient warm water to form a dough which comes together with your hands.

2. Once it forms a ball, turn on to a floured board and knead for about 10 minutes, until the dough feels smooth and silky. Place in a clean, oiled bowl and cover with clingfilm. Put it somewhere warm to rise (I use the airing cupboard). Allow 1 hour at least: it should have almost doubled in size.

2. Once it has risen, roll out, using the heel of your hand, into a round about 10 in/25 cm in diameter and place on a lightly oiled baking tray. Spread the tomato purée over the base, then the pesto. Top with diced goat's cheese and drizzle over the olive oil.

3. Again leave it somewhere warm for 25–30 minutes, until the outside edge is puffed up. Preheat the oven to Gas Mark 8/230°C/450°F. Just before baking, scatter over the whole basil leaves. Bake for 15–20 minutes, until well-risen and golden brown.

NOTE: This is better not frozen.

Fish Soup with Pesto Croûtons

I have to admit there is nothing quite like a bowl of bouillabaisse. There are a number of variations on the theme of this classic Marseillaise dish. Many a proud French housewife lies brazenly about the provenance of her wonderful fish soup, for the jars of bouillabaisse which you can buy from markets, fishmongers or even supermarkets, are so good, that they encourage dishonesty in cooks who would never normally open a tin of soup! All you need to do is reheat the soup (which is made from all sorts of fish and usually the shells of crustaceans, to give a good colour and flavour), then serve, bouillabaisse-style, with rouille and croûtons. In my soup recipe, instead of spreading rouille on the croûtons, I suggest a smear of freshly-made pesto. Then, just before the croûtons submerge into the hearty soup (which is actually more of a stew), you sprinkle over some grated Parmesan cheese. It is a meal in itself. If you want to serve an elongated, French-style meal, then follow with a light salad, and perhaps a more copious cheese course than usual, before some light, refreshing dessert. For the fish, any white fillets will do – I suggest cod or haddock, but coley and ling are also excellent. (serves 6)

Soup
3 tablespoons olive oil
1 lb/500 g potatoes, peeled and diced
1 large onion, peeled and chopped
2 garlic cloves, peeled and chopped
½ teaspoon saffron threads
1 pint/600 ml boiling water
2 lb/1 kg white fish fillets
    (such as cod, coley, haddock)
    cut into large, bite-size chunks
salt, pepper

Pesto croûtons
1 thin French stick (ficelle), cut
    into slices
2 tablespoons pesto
2 oz/50 g Parmesan, freshly grated

1. For the soup, heat the oil in a large saucepan. Add the potatoes, onion and garlic and fry gently for about 5 minutes. Meanwhile, soak the saffron threads in the boiling water for 5 minutes, then add to the pan. Bring back to the boil.

2. Once it is boiling, cook, covered, for about 10–15 minutes, or until the vegetables are just tender, then add the fish, reduce the heat to a simmer and cook, covered, for about 5–10 minutes, or until the fish is just done. (Check after 5 minutes.) Add salt and pepper to taste.

3. While the soup is cooking, place the sliced bread on a baking tray in a preheated oven (Gas Mark 2/150°C/300°F) for about 20–25 minutes, until crisp and a pale golden colour.

4. When the soup is ready, ladle some into the warmed soup bowls. Spread some of the pesto on each croûton, then float 3 croûtons on top of each soup bowl. Offer the Parmesan in a separate bowl, to sprinkle over the pesto croûtons.

NOTE: Do not freeze.

Orange and Basil Pork

The combination of orange, basil and pork works very well indeed. The cut of meat, tenderloin, is very lean so, in order to have succulent and moist meat, you must wrap it well in rashers of streaky bacon and also baste often, with the pan juices while it cooks. Once you have prepared the meat, layering on the garlic, basil and orange, it can be chilled overnight and cooked the following day. This is a dish to suit all palates, for its flavour is good, but not overpowering. It also looks wonderful when sliced – the pork sandwiched around the orange and basil filling – with a topping of crispy, golden bacon. I like to serve this with sautéed potatoes and steamed broccoli or spinach, although a tomato salad would also go well. (serves 4–6)

---

2 pork tenderloins (each about 12 oz/375 g), trimmed
salt, pepper
the grated zest and juice of 2 oranges
20 large basil leaves
4 garlic cloves, peeled and crushed
10 rashers rindless streaky bacon
3 tablespoons olive oil

---

1. Make a deep cut lengthways in each tenderloin. Open them out flat, then season with salt and pepper.

2. Rub the orange zest over the fillets, then lay on the basil leaves, side by side. Sprinkle over the garlic.

3. Carefully roll up the tenderloins, so that the filling is enclosed, then wrap round the rashers of bacon. Secure with cocktail sticks.

4. Put the 2 tenderloins in a shallow dish and pour over the orange juice and 1 tablespoon of the olive oil. Cover with clingfilm and place in the fridge. Leave for at least 4 hours, preferably overnight.

5. Next day, remove the pork and reserve the marinade, discard the cocktail sticks and dry the meat off with kitchen paper. Preheat the oven to Gas Mark 6/200°C/400°F.

6. Heat the remaining 2 tablespoons oil in a frying pan, then add the pork and brown all over, taking great care that the bacon remains wrapped all around.

7. Transfer the tenderloins to a roasting tin, pour over the remaining marinade, and place in the preheated oven for 15 minutes, then reduce the heat to Gas Mark 4/180°C/350°F and roast for a further 25–30 minutes, or until it is cooked through. (Check by piercing the thickest part with a sharp knife). Baste often while it is cooking.

8. Allow the meat to rest, loosely covered with foil, for at least 5 minutes, then cut into slices and serve, with a little of the juices poured over.

NOTE: Do not freeze.

Mushroom and Basil Frittata

If you have ever wondered what to do with leftover pasta, read on. Be sure that the basil is finely chopped, otherwise it will not flavour the entire frittata. I suggest cooking pasta freshly for this, but if you want to use yesterday's spaghetti, then simply warm it up a little with the oil you would toss it in, before adding the eggs and cheese. Eat the frittata warm, or take on a picnic to eat cold. (serves 4)

8 oz/250 g capellini (angel hair pasta)	3 large eggs, beaten
1 tablespoon olive oil	salt, pepper
2 oz/50 g butter	3 heaped tablespoons basil (about
8 oz/250 g mushrooms, thinly sliced	20 large leaves), finely shredded
4 oz/125 g mature Cheddar, grated	

1. Cook the capellini in boiling, salted water until just cooked (only about 2–3 minutes). Drain and toss it in the oil.

2. While the pasta is cooking, heat the butter in a heavy, 8 in/20 cm frying pan and fry the mushrooms for about 5 minutes.

3. While the pasta is still hot, stir in the cheese, eggs, plenty of salt and pepper and then the basil, mixing well. Tip this into the frying pan, on top of the mushrooms, and press down well so that the pan is evenly covered. Cook over a fairly high heat for about 5 minutes. Remove the pan from the heat and place a large heatproof plate over the top of it. Then, holding the frying pan handle with one hand and the plate in the other, quickly turn the pan upside down, so that the frittata is inverted on the plate. Slide it back into the pan, cooked side up, and continue to fry for 8–10 minutes until both top and bottom are golden brown and crispy.

4. Slide the cooked frittata on to a serving plate and allow to cool for at least 20 minutes before cutting into wedges and eating. NOTE: Do not freeze.

Basil and Coconut Muffins

Basil is a fairly sweet-tasting herb and the green flecks and subtle basil flavour match coconut just as well here in a sweet recipe as they do in many Malaysian or Thai hot/spicy recipes. (makes about 10)

<u>Muffins</u>	1 teaspoon cinnamon
2 eggs	½ teaspoon salt
6 fl oz/175 ml milk	3 tablespoons basil leaves, chopped
3 fl oz/90 ml vegetable oil	5 oz/150 g desiccated coconut
8 oz/250 g plain flour	2 oz/50 g chopped hazelnuts
1 level tablespoon baking powder	<u>Topping</u>
2 oz/50 g caster sugar	2 teaspoons demerara sugar

1. Preheat the oven to Gas Mark 6/200°C/400°F. Combine the eggs, milk and vegetable oil. In a separate bowl, sift the flour and baking powder and add the sugar, cinnamon, salt, basil, coconut and hazelnuts. Mix together, then make a well in the centre. Add all the liquids and mix briefly until combined. Do not overwork.

2. Place paper muffin cases in bun tins and fill the cases with spoonfuls. Top with sugar. Bake in the preheated oven for about 20 minutes until well risen. Cool on a wire rack. NOTE: Can be frozen.

chapter 2

bay

I remember, during one of my many stays in France, taking down a recipe for garlic soup, which involved 'laurier'. Without even looking in my dictionary, I translated this as laurel. Only when I had no success finding laurel leaves to flavour my soup, did I realise that another name for bay is bay laurel or sweet bay – *Laurus nobilis*. All became clear: it was bay I needed, not laurel, which is never used in cooking.

Most recipes incorporating bay assume that the cook will use dried leaves. They are perhaps more aromatic, but dried bay leaves do have a 'use-by' date and those which have been hanging around the kitchen for years will have no flavour left. I prefer to use fresh bay leaves for I love their strong scent and bold, yet not overpowering flavour. The following recipes call for fresh bay leaves, some of them require up to six: dried bay would entirely dominate the dish but fresh bay can safely be used in greater quantities.

A native of Asia Minor, bay was established in the Mediterranean at a very early date. Bay thrives best in individual large tubs, filled equally with sand, loam and peat. The soil should never be allowed to dry out. It is very slow-growing, but can reach a height of 40–60 feet.

It was bay which made up the crown of laurel leaves of Ancient Greeks and Romans, who honoured warrior-heroes, emperors and accomplished athletes by crowning them with ceremonial wreaths. Bay was, in fact, so highly regarded by the Greeks, that they dedicated it to Apollo. In Greek myths, Daphne, a nymph who was pursued by Apollo, fled from his advances, only to find herself being changed into a bay tree by the god.

Apart from the ceremonial use of bay in ancient times, it was used in this country as a curative, prescribed for relief of rheumatic complaints, cramp and all sorts of infectious diseases. Bay was carried at weddings and funerals as a protection and blessing. When a bay tree died, it was considered the most dreadful portent of death or impending disaster.

However, bay's sweet aromatic scent and flavour make it more appropriate for the cooking pot than for a bridal bouquet these days. It is one of the few herbs which is equally good with savoury and sweet dishes, although most cooks use it purely for savoury. Its starring role is as an integral part of the bouquet garni, known as 'bundle of sweet herbs' or 'broth posy' in English. It usually consists of three stalks of parsley, a small sprig of thyme and a small bay leaf. Bouquet garni is added to a multitude of dishes, from stews to stocks.

Bay is also added to marinades, pickles, roasts and poached fish. Bay leaves are often placed in a layer of clarified butter, on top of terrines or patés for added flavour and also colour. I would like to see bay being used more in puddings and deserts. Try it as a flavouring in custards (instead of vanilla), in creams and ices. You can store a couple of leaves in a jar of pudding rice, for the most fragrant rice pudding, use bay during the actual cooking of the rice pudding.

Marinated Olives with Lemon and Bay

For one who used to detest olives of all sorts, I still wonder when my love affair began. Was it a sudden flash or was it a gradual awareness of what I was missing. I have a feeling an elongated holiday in southern France had something to do with it. Olives seem to go so well with hot sunshine and drinks under the sun. But I am now so obsessed by them, I serve them before any dinner or supper party ... with one caveat: always put out a little dish for the stones, otherwise people will not come back for more! These olives are full of flavour. They are marinated in best olive oil, bay leaves and strips of lemon. Although they can be eaten after a day or two, they are best after a couple of weeks, you can keep them for up to 6 weeks in a cool place. (fills one ¼ pint/150 ml Kilner jar)

30–35 black olives (preferably kalamata)
4–5 bay leaves
the thinly pared rind of ½ lemon, cut into strips
about 3½ fl oz/100 ml extra-virgin olive oil

1. You can stone the olives if you like, or leave the stones in. Whichever you choose, pop them into a jar and tuck in the bay leaves and lemon rind, layer by layer.

2. Top with just enough oil to cover (but not to ooze out, once you shut the jar).

3. Cover tightly and keep for at least 48 hours, but preferably for at least 7 days, before eating. Use the flavoured oil, once you have eaten all the olives, for tossing into hot pasta: so simple, but what great flavours!

NOTE: Do not freeze.

Lime and Bay Chicken

This is a good dish to make in the summer, because although it can be served warm, it is even better at room temperature. It lends itself, therefore, to relaxed, lazy summer lunches or suppers. I suggest using boneless, skinned chicken thighs, which are now available in supermarkets, but you could substitute chicken drumsticks instead: the bone can remain in, but you should remove the skin. While it cooks, baste regularly, pressing the bay into the chicken as you do so. I like to serve this with lots of pitta or naan bread, to soak into those citrus and bay juices. Although it is not essential, it looks – and tastes – even better when served garnished with 10 to 12 plump black olives. (serves 6)

10–12 boneless, skinless chicken thighs	4 bay leaves
zest and juice of 2 limes	2 tablespoons olive oil
2 garlic cloves, peeled and crushed	salt, pepper

1. Place the chicken in a shallow ovenproof dish. Mix together the lime zest and juice, garlic, bay leaves, oil, salt and pepper and pour over the chicken. Stir well, to coat. Then cover and leave for 1–2 hours.

2. Preheat the oven to Gas Mark 5/190°C/375°F. Place the dish in the preheated oven for about 20–25 minutes, until cooked through. Baste every 5–10 minutes.

3. Serve the chicken either warm or at room temperature, with plenty of the juices poured over.

NOTE: Do not freeze the dish. If using frozen raw chicken, be sure to defrost thoroughly.

Pot Roast Venison with Bay

This is a wonderful dish to serve for Sunday lunch or a dinner party. By cooking it in plenty of stock and wine, the meat becomes so succulent and tender. The vegetables and cooking liquid are then liquidised into a tasty gravy. I prefer using venison on the bone, as I do think the flavour is best. I have suggested using shoulder, but you could alternatively use haunch of venison. The venison I usually buy is farmed. One of the advantages of farmed venison (apart from the fact that it is available all year) is that the age of the beast is never a mystery: the meat is always from young deer, therefore always tender. It is well-hung and so has all the bold, strong flavour of wild venison. If using wild venison, all you can do is marinade for a couple of days, to try to tenderise the meat. I prefer not to, as all you can taste, after marinading for some days, are the strong marinade ingredients: usually red wine and the herbs and spices. Whether you are cooking wild or farmed venison, it is essential to remember that it is a lean meat, and should either be braised in plenty of liquid or roasted at a high temperature for a short time, then allowed to rest, to ensure even cooking. When making the sauce for this dish, you should taste as you add the redcurrant jelly. Add just enough to give a subtle edge of sweetness. If you find it tastes too sweet, add a little lemon juice to sharpen it up. (serves 8–10)

1½ oz/40 g butter	8 juniper berries, crushed in a mortar
5–6 lb/2.25-2.75 kg shoulder	and pestle
of venison, on the bone	½ pint/300 ml dark venison or
salt, pepper	beef stock
2 carrots, peeled and sliced	7 fl oz/200 ml red wine
2 shallots, peeled and chopped	5 bay leaves
8 oz/250 g mushrooms, chopped	2 tablespoons redcurrant jelly

1. Preheat the oven to Gas Mark 5/190°C/375°F. In a large, lidded, ovenproof casserole, heat the butter until hot. Put in the venison and brown it all over. (It is best to turn it using two carving forks.) Season with salt and pepper. Then carefully remove to a plate.

2. In the same casserole, add the carrots, shallots, mushrooms and crushed juniper berries. Stir well, fry gently for about 3 minutes, then add the stock and wine and bring to the boil. Add the bay leaves, stir, then replace the venison. Cover tightly with foil, then with the lid. Place in the centre of the preheated oven for 15 minutes.

3. Then reduce the heat to Gas Mark 3/160°C/325°F and cook for a further 3 hours. After 1½ hours, remove the lid and give the meat a good baste with the liquid. Replace the lid and complete the cooking.

4. When the cooking is finished, remove the meat (very carefully – it is heavy) to a carving board and cover loosely with foil. Allow it to rest for about 15 minutes before carving.

5. Meanwhile, using a slotted spoon, first of all remove the bay leaves and discard. Then, still with slotted spoon, remove the vegetables in the casserole to a liquidiser or food processor, and add a small amount of the liquid. The amount of liquid is variable: basically, you need just enough to help the vegetables blend into a sauce-like consistency, which is not too thick: more like a gravy than a thick sauce. Process until smooth, then push the sauce through a sieve into a clean saucepan.

6. Add the redcurrant jelly. Reheat, season to taste with salt and pepper and, once you are happy with the sweetness and when it is piping hot, pour into a warm jug and serve with the carved venison.

NOTE: Do not freeze.

Wild Duck with Bay and Radicchio

Use only wild duck, which is so much leaner than farmed duck. Mallard is the largest of our wild duck, although teal, which is tiny, is the most common. If using the latter, cut the cooking time by half and allow one teal per person. If you use frozen duck, defrost thoroughly before cooking. The best way is to roast them in a fairly hot oven, then allow them to rest for a considerable length of time. The bay gives a good flavour to the roasting oil, and the radicchio, which is grilled, then sprinkled with orange juice, is a wonderfully sharp-tasting contrast. Serve this with roast potatoes, turnips, parsnips or Jerusalem artichokes. (serves 2–3)

1 wild duck (about 2 lb/1 kg)	Radicchio
salt, pepper	6–8 large radicchio leaves
4 large bay leaves	2 tablespoons olive oil
2 tablespoons olive oil	1 tablespoon freshly squeezed orange juice

1. Preheat the oven to Gas Mark 6/200°C/400°F Salt the duck all over, then prick with a fork. Place 2 bay leaves inside, then rub it all over with 4 tablespoons of oil. Place the remaining oil and bay leaves in a roasting tin, with the duck. Roast in the oven for about 40–45 minutes, basting twice with the bay-flavoured oil.

2. For the radicchio, place the leaves in a wide grill tray. Season with salt and pepper, then drizzle over the oil. Place under a medium grill (not too near the heat) for about 10 minutes, until just cooked and soft, but not black, turning them over once. Remove from the heat and sprinkle at once with the orange juice.

3. The duck is ready when, if pierced with a sharp knife, the juices run pink, (not red, or clear). Remove to a carving board, cover with foil and leave to rest for 15 minutes. Then cut into slices. Place some grilled radicchio onto each serving plate and the duck on top. Spoon over the grill-pan juices. Serve at once.

Bay Roast Potatoes

Everyone loves roast potatoes, and there are so many different ways to cook them. This recipe uses purely olive oil, which becomes wonderfully flavoured with bay. Do not discard the oil after cooking – it forms the perfect cooking medium for sauté potatoes the following day. I like to serve these potatoes with roast corn-fed or free-range chicken and a steamed green vegetable such as broccoli or green beans. Keep basting the potatoes as they roast, to make them crispy and to impart even more of the bay flavour. (serves 4)

2 lb/1 kg unpeeled, small potatoes	3 tablespoons olive oil
(try to choose even-sized potatoes)	salt, pepper
8–10 small bay leaves	

1. Preheat the oven to Gas Mark 5/190°C/375°F

2. Scrub the potatoes – do not peel. Bring them to the boil in salted water and boil for 3 minutes. Drain, refresh in cold water and dry them well.

3. Meanwhile pour the oil into a roasting tin and place in the oven for 3 minutes, until very hot.

4. Toss the potatoes and bay leaves into the oil, ensuring they are well-coated. Season with plenty of salt and pepper, then bake for 45–50 minutes, or until they are tender and golden brown. Drain them on kitchen pepper and serve at once. NOTE: Do not freeze.

Bay Leaf Rice Pudding

Rice pudding is such a simple dish, yet one which is so warming and comforting in winter. This version, flavoured with bay leaves, is baked, allowed to cool, then caramelised under the grill. The result is similar to crème brûlée, but with a rice pudding beneath the crunchy crust. Serve at room temperature. Do not refrigerate: this can cause the crust to go soggy. The soft brown sugar in the pudding gives it a dark colour. If you prefer a whiter result, use caster sugar – but it is not quite so reminiscent of caramel. (serves 6)

¼ pint/150 ml double cream	5 bay leaves
1¼ pint/750 ml milk	2 large eggs, beaten
a pinch of salt	3 oz/75 g soft dark brown sugar
2 oz/50 g short-grain (pudding) rice	1½ oz/40 g demerara sugar

1. Place the cream and milk in a heavy saucepan and slowly bring to the boil, with the bay leaves. Once bubbling, add the salt and rice. Stir, then cover. Reduce the heat and simmer for about 15 mintutes, stirring occassionally.

2. Preheat the oven to Gas Mark 2/150°C/300°F. Beat together the eggs and the brown sugar. Remove the saucepan from the heat. Pour the egg and sugar mixture into it, stirring all the time. Mix well, then pour into a buttered, round 3 pint/1.75 litre oven dish. Place in the oven and bake for 1 hour; stir it once halfway through this time.

3. After the hour, remove the dish and, using a couple of forks, dig out the bay leaves and discard. Smooth over the top and put aside to cool.

4. Once the rice is completely cold, blot off any moisture from the surface, then sprinkle over the demerara sugar, ensuring it is evenly spread. Place the dish under a preheated hot grill for about 2–3 minutes or until the sugar has melted and the topping is dark brown and crunchy.

7. Allow to cool (not in the fridge) and serve at room temperature. NOTE: Do not freeze.

Caramelised Peaches with Bay Ice-cream

The flavour of bay in the ice-cream goes very successfully with peaches which are grilled until they are browned on top and succulent underneath. The dish tastes highly perfumed and delightfully exotic. As with all home-made ice-creams, remember to take it out of the freezer about 30–40 minutes before serving and put it in the fridge to soften. I use an ice-cream maker, but it is not essential: simply pour the mixture into a shallow freezer container and place in the freezer. Every couple of hours tip it into a bowl and beat madly to prevent ice crystals from forming. The result is as good, but you must be around to keep beating regularly. (serves 6)

Ice-cream	Peaches
½ pint/300 ml milk	6 ripe peaches
¼ pint/150 ml double cream	1½ oz/40 g caster sugar
6 large bay leaves	
6 oz/175 g caster sugar	
4 egg yolks	

1. For the ice-cream, place the milk, cream and bay leaves in a saucepan. Bring to the boil, then remove from the heat, cover with a lid and leave for 20–25 minutes.

2. Meanwhile, place the sugar and egg yolks into a heat-proof bowl over a pan of gently simmering water and whisk until thick and pale, then remove the bowl from the heat.

3. Strain the milk mixture into the bowl and whisk well. Tip this into a clean saucepan and, over a fairly low heat, cook for about 5 minutes, stirring constantly, until the custard has thickened slightly and the mixture coats the back of a wooden spoon. Pour into a shallow bowl, cover with clingfilm, pressing it tightly to the surface, and leave until cold.

4. Once the custard is cold, pour it into an ice-cream machine and churn until frozen, or place in the freezer and beat every couple of hours.

5. Preheat the grill. Cut the peaches in half and remove the stones. Place in a grillproof dish, cutside up. Sprinkle the sugar over them and grill until caramelised (about 5 minutes). Serve warm with the bay ice-cream. NOTE: Do not freeze the peaches.

Berry Tarts with Bay Cream

These tarts are made with a buttery, nutty pastry, then lined with a bay-scented cream and topped with mixed summer fruits just before serving. They look splendid and taste divine. Be careful when working with the pastry, it is fairly fragile. If it breaks when rolling out, just patch it together. In order to keep its shape and to prevent it shrinking, try to make it well in advance and refrigerate it overnight. If you do not have time to do this, pop the pastry-lined tart tins in the freezer for half an hour to harden up. You will have enough pastry left over for half a dozen jam tarts. Making the filling is easy; but do make sure you cook it for long enough. I like a mixture of blueberries and strawberries for the topping, but any red or black berries will be just as good. Once they are filled, the tarts should be served at once to avoid the danger of collapse. Both the pastry and the filling can be completely prepared and cooked in advance – though I would not recommend more than 6 hours – and assembled at the last minute. (serves 4)

Pastry	Bay filling
5 oz/150 g plain flour	2 egg yolks
3 oz/75 g icing sugar	2 oz/50 g caster sugar
2 oz/50 g ground hazelnuts	1 oz/25 g plain flour
4 oz/125 g unsalted butter, cubed	½ pint/300 ml milk
approximately 2 tablespoons	4 bay leaves
iced water	2 tablespoons mascarpone

Topping
12 oz/375 g mixed summer berries, sliced if necessary

1. For the pastry, sift the flour and icing sugar into a food processor. Add the ground hazelnuts and process briefly. Put in the butter and process until the mixture resembles breadcrumbs. Turn out into a bowl and add just enough water to bring the dough together into a ball with your hands. Wrap in clingfilm and chill for at least 1 hour. Then roll out ready to line four 4 in/10 cm loose-bottomed tartlet tins. Prick the pastry all over and refrigerate overnight.

2. Next day, preheat the oven to Gas Mark 5/190°C/375°F. Line the tins with foil and baking beans and bake for 15 minutes. Remove the beans and foil. Bake for a further 5–8 minutes, until cooked through. Carefully remove the pastry cases from the tins and allow to cool.

3. Meanwhile, make the filling: in a bowl, mix together the egg yolks, sugar and flour. In a heavy-based saucepan, slowly bring the milk and bay leaves to the boil. Remove from the heat once it bubbles. Very slowly add the egg mixture, whisking constantly. Cook over a low heat for 4–5 minutes, whisking constantly, until the mixture has thickened and there are no lumps. Remove the bay leaves, tip the mixture into a bowl and cover tightly with clingfilm. Chill until needed.

4. Just before serving, mix the Mascarpone into the bay cream, whisking until well blended. Fill the tarts carefully with this cream. Top with the berries. Serve at once. NOTE: Do not freeze.

chapter 3

chervil

Chervil (*Anthriscus cerefolium*) has been far more extensively used in France than Britain. A native to south-eastern Europe and the Middle East, it was, like so many other herbs, introduced to this country by the Romans. It is now also cultivated widely throughout the rest of Europe, in North Africa, North and South America and East Asia.

Chervil is a hardy annual. The seeds germinate very quickly, and so successive sowings from spring through to late summer will ensure a supply of fresh leaves for most of the year. It grows up to 18 inches high, and the fresh, bright green leaves look lacy and fern-like. It prefers a light soil and dislikes being too hot or dry, so a shady area of the garden is most suitable. Window boxes or containers are a good option if there is any chance of frost.

With its feathery, decorative leaves chervil, like parsley, is most frequently used simply as a garnish. Its taste – although delicate, savoury, mildly aniseed and reminiscent of liquorice or even caraway – is quite striking. I think it is wasted simply garnishing a plate, and I recommend using it in cooking.

In the Middle Ages chervil, both leaves and roots, was valued as a medicine. It was reputed to have cleansing properties for the blood, liver and kidneys and was prescribed as a diuretic and for treatment of jaundice. An infusion of chervil and water was also used as an eye-wash, to soothe inflammations or tired eyes and even to reduce wrinkles, particularly around the eyes!

In France chervil is considered one of the most valuable herbs; one of the 'fines herbes' (the others are chives, parsley and tarragon). In Britain we are gradually becoming more aware of the value of its delicate flavour. When finely chopped (or torn), it is excellent with fish, vegetables, eggs or light meats. Since it is not a robustly-flavoured herb, chervil responds better to quick, last-minute cooking. It certainly should not be added to dishes such as stews or casseroles, which have to cook for a long time. It is at its best when added at the very end of cooking, or indeed raw, just before serving.

Classically chervil is used in many French sauces, such as *ravigote*. It is also often added to bechamel and cream-based sauces. It makes a good vinegar, made in the same way as the tarragon vinegar, which can be incorporated into reduced sauces at the last minute or added to vinaigrettes. It makes a very welcome addition to any green salad – tear it over after tossing. Similar to parsley soup, there is a chervil-based soup, often enhanced with cream, which is popular in many parts of Europe and is quite delicious. It works well with most egg recipes, from the simplest of omelettes to a hollandaise sauce: in the latter, it should be stirred in after the sauce has emulsified. Finally, it is splendid with seafood. For a real treat, open half a dozen oysters. Mix together a little dry white wine, chopped shallots, finely chopped chervil and plenty of seasoning. Spoon some of this over each oyster . . . sheer bliss, especially if accompanied by a glass of chilled champagne!

Avocado and Palm Heart Salad

The subtitle of this recipe is Venezuelan Salad, for, apart from Caesar Salad, it is probably the most common salad to be found in Venezuelan restaurants. I used to eat it as a starter, with plenty of the local corn (maize) bread, before sampling one of the country's fine fish dishes. Although it varied marginally from restaurant to restaurant, the basic components are the same: avocado and palm hearts, dressed with olive oil and lime juice. Palm hearts, which can be found in tins in most supermarkets and delicatessens, are known as palmitos in South America. They have the most wonderful smooth, firm texture, which blends beautifully with the soft, creamy avocado. The chervil lifts the flavours with its aniseed taste. I prefer to tear it over at the last minute but, if you prefer, chop it up finely before adding. Serve this as a starter with lots of warm bread, or as a salad to accompany barbecue food. (serves 4)

1 x 13 oz/400 g tin of palm hearts	salt, pepper
1 cos lettuce, washed and torn into large pieces	4 tablespoons olive oil
	1 tablespoon freshly-squeezed lime juice
2 ripe avocados, peeled and sliced	2 tablespoons chervil, chopped

1. First, drain the palm hearts and cut each in half, lengthways.
2. Put the cos lettuce in a bowl, and lay the palm hearts on top, arranged in lines if you like symmetry.
3. Top with the avocado slices, and season with salt and pepper. Drizzle over the oil, then the lime juice, and then, just before serving, top with the chopped chervil.

NOTE: Do not freeze

Chervil-Baked Eggs

In this simple dish, the delicate, slightly aniseed taste of chervil is shown to best advantage. Chervil works perfectly with eggs, as they cook relatively quickly. For this recipe, use medium-size free-range eggs (size 3). The cooking time of 10 minutes gives an egg which is still nicely soft, without being runny. For those who prefer a rather runny yolk, cook for 8 minutes. For a much firmer set, cook for 12 minutes. Ideally, these should be served with a mound of hot buttered toast fingers for dipping into the chervil-flavoured creamy juices. Serve this dish for a light lunch or starter at supper. It can even be served for late breakfast or brunch. (serves 4)

1 oz/25 g butter, softened	2 tablespoons chervil, chopped
4 free-range eggs	4 tablespoons double cream
salt, pepper	

1. Preheat the oven to Gas Mark 4/180°C/350°F. Generously grease four ¼ pint/150 ml ramekins with the butter.
2. Break an egg into each one. Season well with salt and pepper. Top with the chopped chervil.
3. Carefully spoon over the double cream, so that the eggs are completely covered.
4. Place the ramekins on a baking tray in the preheated oven for 10 minutes, or until done to your liking.
5. Serve piping hot, with plenty of toast to dunk.

NOTE: Do not freeze.

Chervil Butter

This is a basic recipe, which can be made with other herbs. Depending on which butter you make, you will need to adjust the herb quantities. For example, if you use a strongly-flavoured one such as sage or tarragon, reduce the amount to 2–3 tablespoons, instead of 4 tablespoons. If, however, you use a more delicate herb, such as marjoram or dill, then you may need to add more. With any herb butter, there are a myriad of uses. The most simple – and possibly most effective – is a topping for grilled meat (steaks or chops) or fish (steaks, fillets or whole fish), or a bowl of freshly cooked vegetables or pasta. You can also use herb butters during the actual cooking process, for example starting off a risotto, searing roast meat or incorporating into a sauce. There are several other ways of using herb butters, as the following recipes will show. The chervil butter is versatile, as it is delicate in flavour, and therefore it complements, rather than dominates, the ingredients it accompanies. If you want to serve slices of the butter atop a piece of grilled steak, roll it, while still soft, into a long round shape, as if you were rolling out plasticine. Then wrap in foil and refrigerate (or freeze) before use.

---

3 oz/75 g unsalted butter, softened
4 tablespoons chervil, finely chopped
1 tablespoons freshly squeezed lemon juice
salt, pepper

---

1. Place the softened butter in a bowl, then beat in the chervil. You can use a mortar and pestle, but I think it works well enough in a bowl, with a wooden spoon.
2. Add the lemon juice, then salt and pepper, combining everything well.
3. Spoon the butter into a small bowl or ramekin and chill until it is firm, then use as necessary.
NOTE: This herb butter freezes well. Defrost for 1–2 hours, before using.

Pitta Toasts

We've done garlic bread to death. But, with the addition of a herb, such as chervil, and only a soupçon of garlic, this flavoured butter can work well with any hot bread. I like to halve mini-pitta breads, which are now available from supermarkets, then spread some of the flavoured butter on top, before baking them in the oven until the butter has soaked into the pitta and the bread has become toasted and almost crispy. Serve them either with aperitifs, as simple appetisers, or as an accompaniment to barbecued food or serve whenever you might ordinarily serve hot garlic bread; it makes a delicious and very welcome change! (makes 12–16 toasts)

6–8 mini-pittas
2 oz/50 g chervil butter
1 garlic clove, peeled and crushed

---

1. Preheat the oven to Gas Mark 6/200°C/400°F. Halve the pittas, horizontally.
2. Soften the chervil butter, then mix in the garlic and combine well.
3. Spread a little of the butter on to each pitta half, and place them on a baking tray.
4. Bake them in the preheated oven for 5–8 minutes, until the butter has melted and they are lightly crisp. Serve at once.
NOTE: Do not freeze.

Salade Niçoise

I have always loved Salade Niçoise, in all its various forms. The basic components are, of course, tuna, anchovies, olives, lettuce, tomatoes, eggs and green beans. Potatoes, artichoke hearts, avocado or sun-dried tomatoes are optional extras. For this salad, instead of using the regular tinned tuna, I have substituted fresh tuna steaks. These are now available in many fishmongers' shops, although frozen steaks will do, at a pinch, when fresh are difficult to find. The taste will be just as good, but the texture will not be quite as firm. The potatoes are firstly fried in olive oil, then the tuna is added to the pan. It is important to tip all the oily juices from the pan into the salad bowl at the end of cooking, for this is what makes the salad dressing, with the help of a little vinegar. Although I prefer the crunchy cos leaves, you can use any other very crisp lettuce. The chervil enhances the strong, almost meaty taste of the tuna very well. All in all, this is a salad packed full of punchy flavours: perfect for lunch on a warm summer's day. Serve with lots of crusty baguette. (serves 4)

1 large cos lettuce, washed
salt, pepper
4 oz/125 g green beans, topped and tailed
5 tablespoons olive oil
8 small new potatoes, scrubbed and boiled until just tender
4 small tuna steaks (or 2 large, divided into 4), about 5 oz /150 g each
4 tomatoes, quartered
2 hard-boiled eggs, peeled and quartered
6 tinned anchovy fillets, drained
12 pitted black olives
1 tablespoon balsamic vinegar
4 tablespoons chervil, chopped

1. Tear the cos lettuce leaves and place in a bowl. Season well with salt and pepper.

2. Cook the beans in boiling, lightly salted water for 2 minutes, then drain and refresh in cold water.

3. In a frying pan, heat 2 tablespoons of the oil, then slice the potatoes into thick slices and fry for about 5 minutes, until golden. Remove the slices to a plate as they cook.

4. Season the tuna. Heat the remaining 3 tablespoons of oil in the same frying pan, then fry the tuna for about 3–4 minutes each side, depending on the thickness.

5. Meanwhile, add the tomatoes, beans and eggs to the lettuce, followed by the potatoes, anchovies, and olives.

6. Once the tuna is cooked, place it on top of the salad, pouring over all the oil. Return the pan to the heat and pour in the vinegar. Bubble for a couple of seconds, then pour it over the salad.

7. Finally, top with the chervil, and serve at once.

NOTE: Do not freeze

Quinoa with Chervil

A little-known grain in this country, quinoa is commonplace in South America. It is reputed to have been a staple of the Incas and it is still grown high in the Andes, in Peru and Bolivia. I use it in many recipes which call for either bulghar wheat or couscous; it can even be used in many rice recipes. The following is a variation on many themes: pilaff, tabbouleh, risotto. As it is a rather bland-tasting grain, it is important to add interesting flavourings. Using the basic measurements in the following recipe, you can add some spices at the first stage of frying – try ground cumin or coriander, or even some chopped chilli, to enliven the dish. Add some extra nuts or seeds, such as chopped hazelnuts, pine kernels or sunflower seeds. Any leftovers can be mixed with a couple of tablespoons of good olive oil, half a tablespoon of wine vinegar and some more chopped chervil for a quinoa salad. Indeed, this recipe could be served cold as a salad. You can be generous with the chervil here, for it is the dominant flavour, and it is also essential for a good colour contrast. Serve as a vegetarian dish or to accompany roast or grilled meat. (serves 4)

6 oz/175 g quinoa
2 tablespoons olive oil
3 shallots, peeled and finely chopped
2 large garlic cloves, peeled and chopped
1 oz/25 g currants
1 oz/25 g flaked almonds
½ pint/300 ml hot light chicken or vegetable stock
4 tablespoons chervil, chopped
salt, pepper

1. Rinse the quinoa well in a colander.

2. Heat the oil in a pan, then gently fry the shallots and garlic for about 3 minutes.

3. Add the quinoa, currants and almonds and stirring well, cook for about 2 minutes.

4. Add the hot stock, bring to the boil, then cover with a tight lid and reduce the heat to a gentle simmer. Cook for about 12–15 minutes, until the liquid is all absorbed.

3. Remove from the heat and stir in the chervil. Season generously with salt and pepper, stir well, then cover and leave to stand for at least 5 minutes before serving.

NOTE: Do not freeze.

Garden Peas with Chervil

Although we resort to frozen peas for most of the year, there is little to rival the pleasure of eating freshly podded garden peas in the summer. They might not taste quite so sweet as frozen peas, but I prefer this. When choosing fresh peas, always avoid wrinkled, dried-looking pods which generally contain tough, old peas. The idea of the shelling process might seem rather tedious, but whenever I actually force myself to do it I find it quite therapeutic. Alternatively, it is a good chore to involve the children in whilst you supervise from afar! Although we are used to serving peas hot, with butter and possibly some chopped mint or dill, this recipe, which is simplicity itself, is quite delicious. By serving them at room temperature, the flavour of the peas comes to the fore, enhanced by the fruitiest of olive oils and the delicately-flavoured chervil. (serves 4)

1 lb/500 g shelled peas (about 2 ½ lb/1.1 kg pods)
3 tablespoons extra-virgin olive oil
salt, pepper
3 spring onions, finely chopped
3 tablespoons chervil, finely chopped

1. Cook the peas in boiling water for 4–5 minutes, until they are just tender.

2. Drain well, then toss in the olive oil. Season to taste with salt and pepper.

3. Allow them to cool to room temperature, then stir in the spring onions and the chervil. Serve at once.

NOTE: Do not freeze.

Chervil-baked Chicken

This dish could also be called Chicken Kiev with a difference. Instead of being deep-fried, as classical chicken kiev dishes are, it is baked in a hot oven. This ensures that there is little danger of the assembled chicken breast collapsing, as it might when deep-fried in Chicken Kiev. The butter is usually flavoured with either parsley or tarragon. I prefer using chervil, for its taste works very well not only with the chicken, but also with the lemon juice, in the butter. The breasts can be prepared several hours in advance, then refrigerated before baking. Although classic recipes use white breadcrumbs which have been dried in the oven, I usually like to use breadcrumbs made from brown bread. You can toast it before using, but I find that the cooking time in the oven gives it a sufficiently toasted flavour and golden colour anyway. It is, however, easier to use bread which is a couple of days old, rather than a soft, fresh loaf. Serve the chicken with buttered noodles or tiny new potatoes, and with some green vegetable, such as spinach or runner beans. (serves 4)

4 boneless chicken breasts, skinned (about 5 oz/150 g each)
2 tablespoons chervil butter
1 large egg, beaten
salt, pepper
2 oz/50 g brown (or white) breadcrumbs (made from 2 day-old bread)
1 tablespoon olive oil

1. Preheat the oven to Gas Mark 6/200°C/400°F. Using a very sharp knife, cut a deep slit into the thick side of each breast, so that you form a pocket.

2. Tuck about half a tablespoon of the chervil butter into each of these pockets.

3. Place the egg in a shallow dish and season well with salt and pepper. Place the breadcrumbs into another shallow dish, alongside.

4. Dip the chicken breasts into the egg, then directly into the breadcrumbs, taking care that the butter remains in place, sealed inside the 'pocket'.

5. Oil a baking tray with the olive oil, then carefully place the four chicken pieces on the tray.

6. Place in the preheated oven for about 25 minutes, or until the chicken is cooked through. Test after 20 minutes by inserting a sharp knife into the thickest part. If the juices run clear, it is ready.

7. Remove the chicken to serving plates, pour over the pan juices and serve at once.

NOTE: Do not freeze.

chapter 4

chives

A well-known and much-loved member of the onion family (*Allium* genus), the mild onion flavour of chives (*Allium schoenoprasum*) makes them an extremely useful garden herb. Chives once grew wild over the cooler parts of the northern hemisphere; from Siberia, through Britain, to Canada. Introduced into China over 2000 years ago, they were used as an antidote to poisoning and as a remedy for bleeding. It is believed that cultivation of the plant did not begin until the Middle Ages. Now it is very rare to find wild species.

Hardy perennials, chives have hollow, thin, grass-like leaves and glorious mauve-purple flowerheads. Chives are not only handy in the kitchen, but decorative in the garden. Although they can be grown from seed, they are more often propagated by dividing.

Chives contain the sulphur-rich volatile oil which is characteristic of all the onion family, and which is mildly antiseptic. Garlic chives are another variety, whose flavour is a remarkable combination of both chive and garlic. These are terrific in salads, where you might ordinarily add some crushed garlic to the dressing. Chives should be cut close to the ground, so they will regrow quickly. The best way is to gather a bunch in your fist, then cut, with a sharp knife or scissors, near to the base of the plant. Chives can be kept in a sealed bag in the salad drawer of the fridge for 2–3 days, or in a jug of water for several hours.

The flowers are useful not only as a substitute for the leaves, where they are to be added towards the end of cooking, but also as a garnish. The best way to tackle them is to hold the flowerhead, blossom upwards, in one hand; and with a pair of scissors in the other, snip a 'V'-shaped cut, with two sharp snips upwards into the blossom. The individual florets will then fall away from the stem, giving you lots of tiny flowers. Use these in salads, butters, soups and vegetable dishes, added at the very end of cooking, to preserve their delicate texture. Their flavour is similar to the leaves, although the flowers of garlic chives are very pungent indeed.

On the whole, freshly chopped chives should be added near the end of cooking, not simply to retain their flavour, but also their bright green colour. They have a natural affinity with egg and cream cheese dishes; mix them with a little cream cheese and add to omelettes. You can make a simple paté by mixing chopped chives with cream or curd cheese and either grated cucumber, lemon and garlic or smoked fish such as trout or salmon. Add them to salads; either tossed in at the end, or mixed into the vinaigrette. They also work well with rice dishes; risottos or salads. Mix with butter or curd cheese for a baked potato filling. Make chive butter by mixing 3 tablespoons of softened unsalted butter with 3 tablespoons finely chopped chives, seasoned with lemon juice, salt and pepper; shape this into a long roll, wrap in foil and freeze. Cut off small sections as you wish to use it; perhaps for topping grilled white fish or barbecued chicken. Do not throw away the chive bulbs either: these can be pickled in vinegar and sugar, then served with cold meats and cheese after maturing for several months.

French Onion Soup with Chive Croûtons

French onion soup is an old favourite. It is also very easy – although not as quick to make as some might think. After initially cooking the onions until they are soft, they must be cooked further, over a fairly high heat, to turn them a golden brown colour. Only by doing this will the soup become a glorious deep brown, not a wishy-washy pale colour. Some cooks pop the croûtons into the actual soup bowls, then place them under the grill. I find it easiest to bake the croûtons in the oven, then place them in the soup just before serving. The chives work very well here, as not only are they a continuation of the onion theme; they also give a good bright flash of colour under the gooingly melted cheese. I always issue warnings before serving this soup; every time I make it, I burn my tongue, because I simply cannot wait. Be warned! (serves 4)

2 oz/50 g butter
1 lb/500 g large onions, peeled, thinly sliced
1 oz/25 g plain flour
1¾ pints/1 litre chicken stock
salt, pepper
croûtons
4 slices of French bread, about ¾ inch/2 cm thick
softened butter
2 tablespoons chives, finely chopped
2 oz/50 g Gruyère cheese, grated

To serve
½ tablespoons chives, chopped

1. Melt the butter in a large saucepan, then fry the onions. Put the lid on the pan and cook over a very low heat for about 20 minutes, until soft.

2. Remove the lid, increase the heat and continue cooking them for about 10 minutes, until the onions are golden brown.

3. Stir in the flour, and cook for 1 minute, stirring constantly, then add the stock and salt and pepper.

4. Bring to the boil, then reduce to a simmer, cover, and cook for about 20 minutes. Taste for seasoning.

5. Meanwhile, make the croûtons. Preheat the oven to Gas Mark 4/180°C/350°F. Butter the bread on one side. Top with the chives and then the cheese. Bake in the preheated oven for about 10–15 minutes, until the cheese has melted.

6. To serve, ladle the soup into 4 soup bowls. Top with the croûtons, then sprinkle over some freshly chopped chives. Serve at once.

NOTE: The soup (without the croûtons) can be frozen. Defrost and reheat gently.

Trout and Chive Paté

This paté is as quick as a flash to make. It is also very tasty. As it freezes well, it can be made in quantities and frozen in small tubs, for later use. I like to serve it with rough oatcakes or hot toast, either as a snack lunch or as canapés, to go with drinks before dinner. It is important to use hot-smoked trout, which resembles smoked mackerel or kipper fillets, rather than the cold-smoked trout available, which is more reminiscent of thin slices of smoked salmon. Be sure to use plenty of seasoning for the paté, as the chive and trout flavours are fairly strong. (serves 4)

6 oz/175 g hot-smoked trout fillets
4 oz/125 g curd cheese
4 oz/125 g fromage frais
the juice and grated zest of 1 lemon
½ oz/15 g chives, chopped
salt, pepper

1. Place the first five ingredients in a food processor and whizz together until well blended. Taste and add salt and pepper accordingly.
2. Tip into a small bowl and either refrigerate for at least 2 hours or freeze for up to 2 months.
3. Serve on large oatcakes or bannocks, or tiny, cocktail-size oatcakes, or with hot toast.

NOTE: The paté freezes well. Defrost thoroughly.

Clapshot

Clapshot is a dish from the Orkneys, very similar to Colcannon from Southern Ireland and Champ in Northern Ireland. Another variation on the theme is one of my mother's dishes, Rumbledethumps, a Lowland Scottish dish. It, too, is a mixture of potatoes, butter and chives but, instead of the turnip of clapshot, there is cabbage. Once mashed, it is placed in an oven dish, topped with grated Cheddar and baked in the oven until the cheese melts. On a cold damp day, I can think of nothing more satisfying than either Rumbledethumps or Clapshot. The latter is the most perfect accompaniment to haggis, as it is a mixture of neeps (turnip) and tatties (potatoes). You can also serve Clapshot with any roast game, sausages, grilled cod and as a topping on a shepherds pie! (serves 4)

1¼ lb/625 g potatoes, peeled, cut
12 oz/375 g turnip (swede), peeled, cut
2½ oz/65 g butter, melted
salt, pepper
2 tablespoons chives, finely chopped

1. Cook the potatoes and turnip in boiling water for about 20 minutes, until cooked.
2. Drain well, then mash with a potato masher. Once thoroughly mashed, add the melted butter and beat well until smooth. Add plenty of salt and pepper, then stir in the chives and serve piping hot.

NOTE: Do not freeze.

Pumpkin and Chive Risotto

I first came across the use of pumpkins in exciting, unusual recipes during a summer stay in Australia. Prior to this visit, I had eaten pumpkin pie, made from tinned pumpkin purée, and cannot say I was greatly enamoured of it. Since I have taken to using pumpkins instead of turnips for the children's Hallowe'en lanterns, I have a lot of pumpkin flesh to use up. Soups are the obvious choice – and a great family favourite. But I also like to grate some into breads and scones; this gives them a delicious moist texture and unusual yellow colour. In Australia, I tried chunks of roast pumpkin with joints of roast or barbecued meat. I also enjoyed pumpkin as a filling for cannelloni and ravioli. Continuing the Italian theme, I often love to make a risotto which is flavoured with chunks of pumpkin. It is made even more delicious by the contrasting pungent flavour of freshly chopped chives. The amount of pumpkin flesh given in the recipe, by the way, is the prepared weight, once you have removed the peel and seeds. For this, you will 1 medium or 3 very small pumpkins (I know this well, for my three children each need a lantern at Hallowe'en!). Butternut squash can be substituted for pumpkins, depending on the season. (serves 6)

2 oz/50 g butter
1 onion, peeled and chopped
1 lb/500 g pumpkin flesh, cubed
12 oz/375 g arborio (risotto) rice
1¾ pints/1 litre hot chicken stock
salt, pepper
1 tablespoon extra-virgin olive oil
3 oz/75 g Parmesan cheese, grated
3 tablespoons chives, chopped

1. Melt the butter, then gently fry the onion until softened. Add the pumpkin and stir to coat in the butter. Cook over a low heat for about 10 minutes.

2. Add the rice, stir to coat, then gradually add the hot stock (the easiest way to keep the stock hot is to have it simmering in a pan alongside your risotto pan). It should be added a ladle at a time, until the rice is just cooked. (You may not need the full amount of stock.)

3. Season to taste with salt and pepper. Stir in the olive oil, then add the Parmesan cheese.

4. Remove from the heat, cover tightly with a lid and allow to stand for 5 minutes. Then remove the lid, mix in the chives and serve at once.

NOTE: The pumpkin flesh can be frozen – so do not feel obliged to cook this only on October 31st!

Potato, Chive and Cheese Pie

This pie is a delightful combination of creamy potatoes, chives, cheese and short crispy pastry. Be sure the pie tin you use is a deep one, otherwise the filling might seep out. I like to use Lancashire cheese, which is one of the better cheeses to cook with. Try to get a farmhouse cheese. I particularly recommend Kirkham's Lancashire, which tastes buttery and tangy. It makes the best Welsh rarebit possible. If you cannot find a farmhouse Lancashire, then a traditionally made Cheddar is also good in this pie. It is the most perfect vegetarian dish; or serve it to accompany a light meat dish, such as grilled chops or cutlets. The difficult thing about this recipe is waiting the quarter of an hour before 'decanting' and cutting-with its golden crust, it looks so inviting. (serves 6)

Pastry
9 oz/275 g plain flour
½ teaspoon salt
5 oz/150 g unsalted butter, cubed
1 egg
1–1½ tablespoons olive oil
1 egg yolk

Filling
2 lb/1 kg potatoes, peeled
6 oz/175 g Lancashire cheese, grated
½ oz/15 g chives, chopped
salt, pepper
2 large eggs
½ pint/300 ml sour cream

1. For the pastry, sieve the flour and salt into a food processor, then add the butter and process until it resembles breadcrumbs. Then add the egg, mixed with 1 tablespoon oil. Process until the dough will come together easily in your hands. You may need to add the extra ½ tablespoon oil. Wrap the dough in clingfilm and chill in the fridge for half an hour.

2. Roll out the dough, on a floured board, to fit a deep, 9½ in/24 cm, loose-bottom pie tin (be sure the pastry comes right up the sides). Prick the pastry base with a fork. Chill the pastry case in the fridge for at least an hour.

3. Preheat the oven to Gas 6/200°C/400°F. Before baking, brush the inside of the pastry case with egg yolk. (This seals the pastry and prevent it becoming soggy.) Bake for 5 minutes.

5. Meanwhile, slice the potatoes as thinly as posible (I use the slicing fitment on my food processor). Cook for 4 minutes in boiling water, then immediately drain and plunge into cold water to stop the cooking. Dry the slices extremely well. (I use several tea-towels for this.)

6. Then, seasoning as you layer, place half the dried potatoes on to the pastry, followed by half of the cheese and then half the chives. Repeat this with the remaining potatoes, cheese and chives. Mix together the eggs and sour cream and pour the mixture slowly over the top of the pie, ensuring that all the edges are covered with liquid. Bake for about 45 minutes, until the pastry is golden and the top is crusty and browned.

7. Remove and wait for about 15 minutes before carefully turning out of the tin. Serve warm, in good size wedges.

NOTE: This does not freeze well.

Pancakes with Smoked Salmon and Chives

In my house these 'Scotch pancakes' were simply called pancakes, but most people call them drop scones, for the obvious reason that the batter is dropped on to a hot griddle to cook. As a child I remember my mother making pancakes at least once a week, on a girdle (the Scottish term for griddle). We would devour these warm, with butter and raspberry or blackcurrant jam or apple jelly. My recipe includes some wholemeal flour, which gives the potatoes a slight nutty, savoury taste, a perfect accompaniment to the smoked salmon and chive cream, which tops it. They are best served warm, either as a simple starter, or – even better – as what caterers call 'finger-buffet' food, to go with drinks. If you want to make the pancakes in advance, simply reheat in a low oven, well wrapped in buttered foil. You can also freeze and reheat gently just before serving. (makes 16–20 pancakes)

Pancakes	Topping
3 oz/75 g self-raising flour	¼ pint/150 ml crème fraîche
1 oz/25 g wholemeal self-raising flour	2 tablespoons chives, finely chopped
½ teaspoon salt	1 teaspoon horseradish relish
1 egg	salt, pepper
½ pint/150 ml milk	4 oz/125 g smoked salmon, in
butter, for frying	thin slices

1. For the pancakes, sieve the flours and salt together, then beat in the egg. Gradually add the milk and whisk well, until there are absolutely no lumps and it is smooth.

2. Heat a griddle or large heavy frying pan and lightly butter it using kitchen paper. Test the griddle by dropping a teaspoon of the batter on to the surface. If it bubbles within a minute, the griddle is hot enough. Drop about 4 dessertspoons of the batter on to the griddle and cook on one side until you see the bubbles start to form. With a palette knife or fish slice, flip over and cook on the other side. When you press lightly on the pancakes and no batter oozes out, then they are cooked. Remove to a wire rack and cover with a cloth. Continue until you have used up all the batter.

3. For the topping, mix the crème fraîche with the chives, horseradish, salt and pepper to taste.

4. To serve, place the warm pancakes on to a plate. Spoon on some of the chive cream, then top with a small sliver of smoked salmon.

NOTE: The pancakes freeze well.

Salmon with Lentils and Chives

Puy lentils are French lentils which hold their shape well once cooked. Unlike the average orange lentil, which are perfect for soups, the Puy lentils do not dissolve into a mush once cooked. They are, therefore, ideal for salads, which should be dressed while still warm, to absorb the flavours thoroughly. I like the combination of salmon with lentil salad. The salmon in this recipe is grilled, but it is also easy to roast in a very hot oven (for this size of fillet, at Gas Mark 9/240°C/475°F, they would only take about 5–6 minutes to cook). If you are lucky enough to have some chive flowers, then do toss them into the salad just before serving, as their colour brightens up the brown lentils; they also make a good garnish to the salmon. The dish is ideal served warm, not hot or cold, so plan on cooking the lentils about 45 minutes before eating time. Start grilling the salmon about 15 minutes before serving up. (serves 4)

8 oz/250 g Puy lentils, rinsed
salt, pepper
1 teaspoon wholegrain mustard
1 tablespoon lime juice
5 tablespoons extra-virgin olive oil
4 tablespoons chives, chopped
4 x (skinless) salmon fillets, about 5–6 oz/150–175 g each
½ oz/15 g butter

1. Bring a pan of salted water to the boil, then tip in the washed lentils. Simmer them for about 15–20 minutes, until just cooked (start testing them after 15 minutes). Drain them, rinse in cold water, then be sure they are completely dry before mixing with the dressing.

2. In a screw-top jar, shake together the mustard, lime, oil, chives and plenty of salt and pepper. Pour this over the lentils and stir well to coat.

3. To cook the salmon, dot the butter over the salmon fillets, then place them on a lightly buttered grill tray. Place under a preheated grill for about 3–4 minutes each side, depending on how thick they are.

4. To serve, spoon a bed of lentils on to plates, then top with the salmon fillets. If you have any chive flowers, scatter the florets over the fish just before serving.

NOTE: Do not freeze.

Strawberry and Chive Salad

Strawberries are not only for desserts! They are good in salads or in chilled soups. In this recipe, they are combined with a very special dressing and flavoured with plenty of freshly snipped chives. Since they look so colourful, I like to serve them with radicchio, that wonderfully red, bitter-tasting, salad leaf. Do not panic when you see champagne included in the list of ingredients – you do not need to get out the vintage Krug! Any dry sparkling wine will do – you can even use dry fizzy cider. It is important to prepare the dressing just before serving, so you still get the effect of those wonderful bubbles! Since strawberries are often taken in conjunction with fizz, this recipe is not as implausible as you might think! Make this salad for any summer celebration. You will have many compliments. (serves 4)

1 head of radicchio
1 lb/500 g strawberries, hulled
2 tablespoons champagne or sparkling wine
2 tablespoons extra-virgin olive oil
salt, pepper
2 tablespoons chives, chopped

1. Wash and roughly tear the radicchio leaves and place around a large, flat serving plate.

2. Slice the strawberries and strew over the top.

3. Just before serving, mix together in a bowl the champagne, olive oil and salt and pepper, then stir in the chives. Pour over the salad and serve straight away.

NOTE: Do not freeze.

chapter 5

coriander

Coriander (*Coriandrum sativum*) was originally native to the eastern Mediterranean, but now it is widely found all over Asia, India and parts of both North and South America. It is one of the most ancient herbs, mentioned in the book of Exodus (16:31) in the Old Testament. Moses and the people of Israel, during their time in the wilderness were provided daily with manna, which had a rather divine taste: 'Now the house of Israel called its name manna; it was like coriander seed, white, and the taste of it was like wafers made with honey.'

A hardy annual, coriander is easily grown in a light rich soil, preferably in full sun. If it is to be grown for the seeds, it should be sown in the early spring, then harvested in the late summer, once the seeds have ripened. If it is to be grown for the leaf (and it is the leaf which is required in the following recipes), then it should be sown in succession throughout the summer.

According to Chinese beliefs, coriander seeds had the power of bestowing immortality. It is now popular as a cooking herb and spice from Peru through Egypt, to the Far East, particularly Thailand. Its seed has been well known as a spice for many years but it is only comparatively recently that the coriander leaf has entered British kitchens and it has certainly taken them by storm. Coriander root is also used in South-East Asian cookery.

The taste of the bright green, shiny leaves is highly aromatic and decidedly addictive; when you start cooking with fresh coriander, you might begin by buying the odd packet or two, you will end up seeking out the Indian and Eastern food shops in Britain, where coriander is sold not in tiny packets, but in vast bunches, like flowers, so much of it is needed in Indian and Eastern dishes. It adds a great deal of flavour to curries and it is combined with chillies and coconut in Far Eastern dishes, often with the addition of lemongrass and one of the fish-based sauces such as 'nam pla'. The leaves are rather reminiscent of flat parsley; in fact, it is often referred to as Chinese parsley. It can be used as generously as parsley in cooking.

Coriander works well with ingredients normally associated with oriental cooking, but also with many of our indigenous ones. You can make a coriander pesto, similar to Ligurian (basil) pesto, and spread a layer on top of either a pheasant breast or a salmon fillet, then roast in a very hot oven, until the meat or fish is just cooked and the pesto has become a golden crust. Or chop some, instead of parsley, into creamy fish pie, with either a potato or pastry topping. It also goes well with common British vegetables such as parsnips, potatoes or cauliflower. Make a flavoured butter with chopped coriander and grated lime juice, then use this to top grilled lamb or barbecued shellfish. It also enhances many salads, from rice or pasta salad, to plain tomato or cos lettuce salads. Dips and 'spreads' such as hummus or tzaziki are also excellent with chopped fresh coriander, as are all varieties of nuts. It makes one of the prettiest garnishes, with its shiny, frilly leaves, so be sure to keep some back when chopping coriander into your sauce or soup, to decorate your dish just before serving.

Chicken Satays

I have always loved anything to do with peanut butter; I eat it on toast for breakfast every day. So a favourite sauce of mine is the peanut sauce to accompany that delicious Malaysian/Indonesian dish, satay (saté). Instead of using chicken breasts, it can be made with rump beef, pork tenderloin or lean cubes of lamb. The idea is to marinate the meat overnight (or for at least 4 hours) to tenderise and flavour, then make a peanut butter-based sauce, to dip the satay sticks into. You should, in theory, use customised wooden sticks for the meat, but if you have not got any, then regular metal skewers will do. Serve the meat and sauce with a crisp fresh salad of lettuce and shallots and offer warmed flat bread alongside. (serves 4)

4 small boneless, skinless, chicken breasts, cubed
3 tablespoons light soy sauce
1 tablespoons lemon juice
1 tablespoon runny clear honey

Sauce
2 tablespoons groundnut oil
2 garlic cloves, peeled and crushed
½ tablespoon chilli sauce
1 tablespoon 'nam pla' (Thai fish sauce)
6 oz/175 g crunchy, sugar-free peanut butter.
½ pint/300 ml water
1 tablespoon lemon juice
4 tablespoons coriander, chopped
pepper

1. For the chicken, mix the soy sauce, lemon juice and honey together. Then add the chicken cubes, stir well and cover. Place in the fridge overnight.

2. For the sauce, heat the oil in a saucepan, then add the garlic and fry gently for about 2 minutes.

3. Then increase the heat and add the chilli sauce, nam pla, peanut butter, water and lemon juice. Stir or whisk until well blended, then lower the heat and simmer for about 10 minutes.

4. Meanwhile, remove the chicken from the marinade, reserving the marinade for later and thread on to wooden sticks or skewers (about 4–5 pieces on each). Place these under a preheated grill.

5. After the sauce has simmered for 10 minutes, add the remaining marinade and bring to the boil. Boil for about 5 minutes, then remove from the heat and add the coriander. Stir well. Season to taste with pepper (you probably will not need salt).

6. Preheat the grill and grill the chicken skewers for about 4–5 minutes each side. Check that the meat is cooked through, by removing one piece and cutting into it with a sharp knife.

7. Serve the satay sticks on a plate, and offer the peanut sauce (which should be barely warm, or at room temperature), in a bowl, to dip into.

NOTE: Do not freeze.

Cauliflower with Coriander

This is a variation on a classic dish, Cauliflower Polonaise, which is topped with fried breadcrumbs, egg and parsley. Since the flavour of coriander goes beautifully with cauliflower (and broccoli), I think this version is a lovely dish to serve, instead of that old favourite Cauliflower Cheese. It also looks rather spectacular, the crunchy breadcrumbs flecked with green coriander and chopped hard-boiled egg. In Finland, there is a recipe for beetroot salad, which is topped with hard-boiled egg. For this dish, the egg yolk is pushed through a sieve, then the yolk is placed neatly along one side of the salad. The white of the egg is finely chopped and placed alongside. The result is a wonderful colour contrast, with the purple beetroot and the white and yellow of the egg. So if you have time, separate the yolk from the white and arrange in lines. Since you are serving the cauliflower hot, however, you have to work pretty quickly. Whichever way you choose to serve the egg, be sure not to overboil it, so its texture is dry and almost powdery. I like a hard-boiled egg which is verging on the soft-boiled! You must make sure it is completely cold before chopping. Serve this splendid-looking dish with roast beef or pork, or as a vegetarian main course. (serves 4)

1 large cauliflower, trimmed, and left whole
2 oz/50 g butter
3 oz/75 g brown breadcrumbs
salt, pepper
2 heaped tablespoons coriander and chopped
1 large egg, hard-boiled and chopped

1. Place the cauliflower in boiling salted water and cook until just done (about 10–15 minutes). Then drain well.

2. Meanwhile, heat the butter in a frying pan and add the breadcrumbs. Fry for 5–10 minutes, or until they are golden brown and crunchy. Allow to cool for about 5 minutes.

3. Season the breadcrumbs with salt and pepper, then add the coriander and stir well.

4. Place the cauliflower on a serving dish, then pour over the coriander breadcrumbs. Top with the chopped egg and serve at once.

NOTE: Do not freeze.

Mango and Coriander Salsa

At summer barbecues or patio suppers refreshing and tangy salsas are becoming more familiar. Little wonder, for they are excellent accompaniments to grilled and barbecued food. This salsa is made with fresh, ripe mango, red onion and coriander. There is a little fiery edge provided by a fresh green chilli, but, as in other recipes with chillies, try only half of the amount suggested, then add more if it is not hot enough: chillies vary so much in strength. The salsa is best made about an hour before serving, so the flavours have time to combine. It should be served at room temperature, with grilled meats, such as pork, lamb or beef or with barbecued seafood such as monkfish, tuna or prawns. This sort of recipe, simple, yet so tasty, is what summer eating is all about. (serves 6 as an accompaniment)

2 large ripe mangoes, peeled, stoned and cubed	2 oz/50 g coriander, roughly chopped
1 red onion, peeled and chopped	½ green chilli, deseeded, very finely chopped
the juice of 1 lime	salt, pepper

1. Combine all the ingredients in a bowl and allow to stand for about 1 hour, before serving.

NOTE: Do not freeze.

Coconut and Chicken Soup

The combination of coconut, coriander and lemongrass is classic in Far Eastern soups. I have decided to omit the tempting addition of hot, fiery red chillies, as I like the gentle, aromatic flavour of the soup as it is. This fragrant soup is quick and easy. You simply need a can of coconut milk, chicken stock, some lemongrass and two chicken breasts. At the end you stir in plenty of freshly chopped coriander and lime juice. Instead of adding salt, add nam pla (Thai fish sauce) to taste. Start off by adding half a tablespoon, then add extra if you want a more pronounced flavour, but do remember, it is very salty. It is important not to overcook the chicken. Only add for the final 5 minutes or so of cooking – the result will be succulent, tender meat. (serves 4)

¾ pint/450 ml chicken stock	4 tablespoons coriander, chopped
1 x 14 fl oz/400 ml tin of coconut milk	juice of 1 lime
1 plump stalk of lemongrass	½–1 tablespoon nam pla (Thai fish sauce)
2 boneless, skinless, chicken breasts, cut into slivers	pepper

1. Place the stock and coconut milk in a saucepan and bring to the boil.
2. Cut off the coarse outer leaves and trim off the base and top from the lemongrass. Chop it very finely indeed, then add to the soup. Allow the soup to boil for about 5 minutes, then add the slivers of chicken breast. Reduce the heat to a simmer, cover and cook for 5 minutes.
3. Check that the chicken is cooked and remove from the heat. Add the coriander and lime juice, then add the nam pla, to taste. Finally stir in some pepper and taste again, adding more nam pla if required.
4. Serve at once, in warmed soup bowls.

NOTE: Do not freeze.

Fish with Tortilla Crust and Mexican Salsa

This is a dish for adults only! Not only is the salsa very hot, from the fresh chilli, but it also has the most wonderful underlying tastes of Mexico: tequila has a strong flavour, which suits the other bold ingredients in the recipe. There is the fresh coriander, a little ground cumin, lime juice, and then some tomatoes are stirred in at the end, to quench the fiery heat! The fish is coated not in the usual plain breadcrumbs, but in a mixture of breadcrumbs and ground tortilla chips. I buy the plain ones, for the chilli-flavoured ones are too spicy for this already well-spiced dish. The end result is a crunchy fish, with a subtle tortilla flavour, which is served with the coriander and Tequila salsa. I like to serve this with a plain tomato salad, dressed only with fruity olive oil, and a large bowl of tortilla chips. Sour cream can also be offered, to contrast with the hot chillies. Since all chillies vary in heat, I suggest adding only half a chilli first, then taste. If it is hot enough for you, then stop there. Otherwise, add the other half, but expect your guests to drink copiously; preferably water, not tequilas! (serves 4)

12–16 tortilla (corn) chips (about ¾ oz/20 g)
2 oz/50 g fresh breadcrumbs
4 medium skinless fillets of cod (or haddock or halibut), about 5 oz/150 g each
1 large egg, beaten

Salsa
2 tablespoons tequila
2 oz/50 g cos lettuce, washed and shredded
3 oz/75 g coriander
½–1 green chilli, deseeded and chopped
1 teaspoon ground cumin
6 tortilla chips
the juice of 1 lime
2 tablespoons sunflower oil
salt, pepper
2 large tomatoes, diced

1. Preheat the oven to Gas Mark 5/190°C/375°F. Place the tortilla chips in a food processor and process until they resemble crumbs. Add the breadcrumbs, then tip on to a plate.

2. Dip the fish fillets carefully into the beaten egg, then press into the tortilla crumbs. Turn them over, so that they are covered all over with the crumbs. Place the fillets on a lightly oiled oven tray and bake at the top of the preheated oven for about 10–15 minutes, until the fish is cooked through and the crust is golden brown.

3. Meanwhile, prepare the salsa: place the first 8 ingredients in a food processor and process until well blended. Add salt and pepper to taste, then spoon into a bowl and stir in the tomatoes. Taste and check the seasoning again.

4. Serve the fish, straight from the oven, with a couple of spoons of the salsa. Offer tortilla chips to go with the fish.

NOTE: Do not freeze.

Lemongrass and Coriander Fishcakes

In Far Eastern recipes, coriander is often combined with lemongrass in fish, meat and vegetable dishes. Here, they flavour chunky fishcakes, which are golden crispy brown outside, moist and tasty inside. I like to use mostly cod or haddock for the main fish, with some crabmeat. Brown meat is usually cheaper and I prefer the colour it gives to the fishcakes, but if you can only buy white crabmeat, then that is fine. As indicated in the freezer instructions, these can be made well in advance, but do ensure that, if you are freezing them, the fish and crab have not been previously frozen. Serve the fishcakes with a tangy sauce, made from yoghurt, capers, lime and coriander. (makes 6)

Fishcakes
1 lb/500 g potatoes (weight after peeling), cubed
12 oz/375 g cod or haddock fillet
¼ pint/150 ml milk, for poaching
4 oz/125 g brown crabmeat
2 oz/50 g butter
4 spring onions, chopped
2 stalks lemongrass, outer layers and coarse tops removed, very finely chopped
2 tablespoons coriander, freshly chopped
juice of ½ lime
salt, pepper
1 egg, beaten
4 oz/125 g fresh brown breadcrumbs
flour
sunflower oil, for frying

Sauce
7 fl oz/200 ml natural yoghurt
1 heaped tablespoon capers, chopped
grated zest of 1 lime
2 teaspoons freshly chopped coriander

1. Boil the potatoes in salted water until just cooked. Drain well.

2. Poach the fish in the milk until just cooked (about 3 minutes). Drain well. Cut into chunks.

3. Add the crabmeat and butter to the potatoes and mash well, with a potato masher. Stir in the spring onions, lemongrass, coriander and lime juice. Combine. Salt and pepper to taste. Gently fold in the chunks of the fish.

4. Form into 6 fishcakes: place a 3 in/8 cm muffin ring or pastry cutter on a plate and fill it with the mixture, packing well in. Then remove the ring and continue with the others. Refrigerate for at least 2 hours.

5. Prepare a plate of beaten egg and one of breadcrumbs. Take the fishcakes and lightly dredge them with flour, dip in the egg, and then in the breadcrumbs. Refrigerate again for 1 hour.

7. Meanwhile, prepare the sauce by thoroughly combining all the sauce ingredients.

8. Preheat the oven to Gas Mark 3/160°C/325°F. Shallow-fry the fishcakes, in a little oil, for 3–4 minutes, until golden brown all over, turning them over very carefully. Remove to the oven for about 25–30 minutes (35–45 minutes if frozen) and serve piping hot, with the sauce.

NOTE: Freeze the fishcakes after stage 6 for up to 2 weeks. Then fry, without thawing, as normal. Bake in the oven for 10–15 minutes longer than required (about 35–45 minutes).

Griddled Pork with Hazelnut, Chilli and Coriander Sauce

The sauce to accompany the pork is a variation on the Spanish classic Romesco Sauce (from the Tarragona area), which is usually served with either fish or chicken. I particularly like it with freshly seared tuna. But it is also excellent with cauliflower, broccoli or celery, or with pork, which I like to cook on a cast-iron griddle. If you do not possess one, use a large, heavy-based frying pan, but oil the meat, rather than the pan. It is essential to have the pan (or griddle) very hot indeed, before adding meat. It will smoke rather a lot, but you must be brave. This is the only way to achieve a well-seared meat, or indeed fish: use the same method for fresh tuna steaks. The sauce can be made a couple of hours in advance and simply brought to room temperature as you cook the meat; it should never be served straight from the fridge. (serves 8)

1 fresh green chilli, cut in half, deseeded
1 large tomato, halved
2 large garlic cloves, peeled but left whole
3½ oz/100 g blanched hazelnuts
7 fl oz/200 ml plus 2 tablespoon olive oil
1 egg yolk
4 heaped tablespoons coriander
1 tablespoon balsamic vinegar
8 pork steaks or chops

1. First make the sauce. Preheat the oven to Gas Mark 5/190°C/375 F. Place the chilli, tomato, garlic and nuts on a baking tray, with 1 tablespoon of the oil. Roast in the oven for about 20 minutes, until the vegetables are just tender. Then remove and tip everything into a food processor. Process briefly, until well blended. Allow to cool in the processor bowl for about 20 minutes.

2. When cold add the egg yolk and the coriander, then process for about 20 seconds. Slowly, with the machine running, add the 7 fl oz/200 ml olive oil, as if making mayonnaise, drop by drop at first, then gradually form a thin stream.

3. Once the oil is all added, tip the contents into a bowl and stir in the vinegar. Taste for seasoning and keep to one side, while you cook the meat.

4. Pat the pork dry with kitchen paper, then rub the remaining tablespoon of oil all over. Allow the griddle or frying pan to heat up until it is very hot indeed. Then add the meat and cook for about 5 minutes on either side, depending on the thickness.

5. Serve at once, with the sauce.

NOTE: Do not freeze.

Spinach and Nut Curry

This is a very rich dish, only to be consumed by nut-lovers. It has wonderful flavours, which are all enhanced by the addition of the coriander at the end. For the nuts, I would recommend either brazil nuts or unsalted cashews, but it is a good idea to halve them into manageable sizes. The addition of the spinach makes a good contrast to the crunch of the nuts. You do not need to use young tender leaves of spinach for this, as you would for a raw spinach salad, use those large, more mature leaves, because they are to be shredded into the curry. As they are only cooked for a couple of minutes they retain their fresh green colour. Since this is very filling, you can offer Basmati rice with it, but I prefer some warm naan bread, to be dunked greedily into the creamy sauce. A little green salad lightly dressed in oil and lemon is a good idea, to serve as an accompaniment. (serves 4)

2 oz/50 g butter
1 large onion, peeled and chopped
½ tablespoon garam masala
½ tablespoon curry powder
6 cardamom pods
1 x 13 oz/400 g tin of coconut milk
3½ oz/100 g creamed coconut
6 oz/175 g brazil nuts or unsalted cashew nuts, halved
salt
6 oz/175 g fresh spinach leaves, washed and shredded
4 tablespoons coriander, chopped

1. Heat the butter in a saucepan and gently fry the onions for about 5 minutes. Then add the garam masala and curry powder.

2. Remove the outer husks from the cardamom pods and tip the little black seeds into a mortar. Grind them with a pestle, then add to the saucepan. Fry for about 2 minutes.

3. Add the coconut milk and bring to the boil, then stir in the creamed coconut. Cover and cook over a gentle heat for about 10 minutes, stirring from time to time.

4. Then add the nuts, and a good grinding of salt. Cover and cook for a further 10 minutes, then add the spinach. Cook, uncovered, for about 3 minutes.

5. Remove from the heat and stir in 3 tablespoons of the coriander. Taste for seasoning, and serve, with the remaining 1 tablespoon of coriander sprinkled on top.

NOTE: Do not freeze.

chapter 6

dill

Dill has a dual purpose: like coriander, it is used not only for its feathery, thread-like leaves, but also for its seeds. The seeds are used as a strong flavouring, particularly for pickles; and they are also, along with fennel seeds, made into gripe water to soothe crying babies. The herb, however, has a far greater range of uses, both culinary and medicinal.

Dill (*Anethum graveolens*) is a hardy annual, which can grow up to 2–3 feet in height. As indicated, all parts of the plant are aromatic, with a clean, sharp, but also sweet flavour. The leaves are very similar to fennel, but the actual dill plant is much smaller. Although both herbs taste of aniseed, and both are associated mostly with fish, dill is more delicate than fennel. Dill is easily grown from seed, preferably in good garden soil, in a sunny and sheltered position.

Although it is a native of India, Russia and southern Europe, it is in northern Europe that it is nowadays most popular. In Scandinavia, in fact, I find that the use of dill in cooking and as a garnish, is often overdone. It is popular in Germany, in central European countries such as the Balkans and Rumania, and in both Turkey and Iran. So it is not, as I had often thought, simply a cold-weather herb. It works beautifully in hot, spicy foods, such as middle-eastern rice pilaffs and tabboulehs.

The word dill is from the old Norse 'Dilla', which means to lull. So it is probable that dill water has been used to quieten unsettled babies since ancient times. It was also prescribed for indigestion and as a tranquilliser. The Greeks used it as a perfume and an incense. It was the Romans who took it to Britain, where it came to be used as a lucky charm. In the Middle Ages brides in some European countries believed it to be good luck to wear a sprig of dill and some salt in their shoes.

Perhaps the dish most often linked with dill is the famous Scandinavian 'Gravadlax', which is an old method of preserving salmon throughout the winter. There are many differing recipes but usually the raw salmon is sprinkled with dill, salt, pepper and sugar, weighted down and left for 3–4 days before being sliced and served with a dill and mustard sauce. I remember watching Finnish friends actually burying a salmon, preserved in the dill mixture, and weighted under heavy stones. The soil acted as a fridge, keeping it cool, and the stones were ideal as weights to bring out the best flavour.

As we are all aware, dill works very well with fish, particularly in creamy or buttery sauces to accompany all sorts of fish, from herring to prawns. It tastes good when chopped into salads, especially with vegetables such as cucumbers and with sour cream or yoghurt dressings. It is used in pickles, particularly for cucumbers, gherkins and cauliflowers. In middle-eastern recipes dill is often used in conjunction with lamb, rice and also spinach. Its flavour is best when it is added towards the end of cooking; although sometimes it is necessary to incorporate dill at the beginning and stir in some more, freshly chopped, just before serving.

Parsnip, Potato and Dill Gratin

This is a wickedly rich dish, definitely neither low in fat nor calories. It is a dish either to serve with something fairly plain – steamed or grilled fish or lamb chops, or to savour entirely on its own. Having eaten so many dill-laden potato dishes in Scandinavia, I thought it might also work with parsnips. I believe I was right! The combination of parsnips and potatoes with freshly chopped dill is splendid. The addition of double cream makes the whole dish luscious and creamy. It is important, with any sort of gratin, to allow it to stand, before serving. I would suggest at least 10 minutes, after which time it is slightly firmer. In the unlikely event of there being any leftovers, pop it back in the fridge and reheat in a medium oven the following day, loosely covered in foil. Garnish with some fresh sprigs of dill, if you like. (serves 6)

1¼ lb/625 g potatoes, peeled
1¼ lb/625 g parsnips, peeled
1 pint/600 ml double cream
2 teaspoon salt
freshly ground pepper
4 tablespoon dill, freshly chopped
½ oz/15 g butter

1. Slice the potatoes and parsnips very thinly. (I do this with the slicing fitment on my food processor; otherwise, use a very sharp knife and cut as thinly as possible). Place them all in a large saucepan with the cream.
2. Add the salt, bring slowly to the boil and simmer for 2–3 minutes, stirring carefully (try not to break up the vegetable slices, but stir well enough, so it does not stick to the bottom).
3. Remove from the heat, grind over plenty pepper, then stir in the dill.
4. Tip the entire contents into a buttered gratin dish (shallow oven-proof dish) and level the surface out roughly. Dot the butter over the top.
5. Bake in a preheated oven (Gas 4/180°C/350°F) for about 60 minutes, or until the vegetables are tender and it is golden brown on top.
6. Allow to stand for about 10 minutes, then serve.

NOTE: Do not freeze.

Dill and Cheddar Muffins

These muffins are good to serve with soups or salads, or on their own, as they have so much flavour. It is important to use a mature Cheddar, to match the dill's strong flavour. I like to use either Isle of Mull or Quicke's Cheddar. When making any muffins, it is important not to overwork the mixture too much. It will look rather a mess when you decant it into the bun cases, but do not worry – they sort themselves out while baking! The muffins are not as huge as the American ones I love eating for breakfast, when I visit the States. Mine are made in paper cases, which I use for fairy cakes for the children. The American versions are so vast they keep you going all day. Usually they are sweet, but I rather like savoury muffins, which are not dissimilar to our cheese scones, but much lighter in texture. (makes about 16)

Muffins
8 oz/250 g plain flour
1 level tablespoon baking powder
salt, pepper
4 oz/125 g mature Cheddar, grated
2 tablespoons dill, freshly chopped
a pinch of cayenne pepper
1 egg
8 fl oz/250 ml milk
2 oz/50 g butter, melted

Topping
1 oz/25 g Cheddar, grated

1. Sift the flour and baking powder together into a bowl, then season with plenty of salt, a little pepper, then add the cheese, dill and cayenne. Make a well in the centre of the bowl.
2. Whisk the egg, milk and butter together, then pour into the well. Work quickly together with a knife, to mix, then spoon the mixture into about 16 bun cases. Top with the remaining cheese.
3. Bake at Gas 5/190°C/375°F for about 20 minutes, or until well risen and golden on top.

NOTE: These freeze well.

Potato Salad with Dill

The first time I ate dill was in Denmark. It was tossed over a dish of hot, boiled potatoes with some butter. Having only ever encountered mint or parsley on potatoes I thought the idea unusual but very good indeed. So now I often chop dill over new potatoes to serve hot. Almost better, however, is to incorporate lots of freshly chopped dill into a potato salad. Potato salads often have a bad name, especially if they are laced with yellow salad cream and have been sitting around at buffets for hours on end. On the other hand, a freshly made one, with good mayonnaise, is a delight. This version has a tangy citrus dressing, which is made more colourful and tasty by the addition of the dill. (serves 4–6)

1½ lb/750 g small new potatoes, scrubbed
the juice and zest of 1 large lemon
3 tablespoons dill, chopped
4 spring onions, chopped
¼ pint/150 ml natural yoghurt
2 tablespoons mayonnaise
salt, pepper

1. Place the potatoes in a pan of cold, salted water, bring to the boil and cook for about 10 minutes, or until tender.
2. Drain well, then toss in the lemon juice and zest. Cool to room temperature.
3. Then whisk together the dill, spring onions, yoghurt and mayonnaise in a bowl. Season with salt and pepper.
4. Pour this over the potatoes and gently combine, using 2 spoons. Take care not to break up the potatoes. Serve at room temperature.

NOTE: Do not freeze.

Couscous with Pecans and Dill

I adore couscous, whether it is served Moroccan-style, with a spicy meat and vegetable stew, or as a salad, tabbouleh-style, with plenty of freshly chopped mint and parsley. This recipe is for a dish of hot couscous enhanced by crunchy pecans which have been toasted, to bring out the full flavour, and lots of dill. It is very simple, yet so effective. Serve it either as a side dish to accompany grilled lamb or roast chicken, or as part of a range of hot dishes at a hot winter buffet. Walnuts are a good substitute for the pecans. (serves 4)

½ pint/300 ml water
2 tablespoons olive oil
7 oz/200 g couscous
salt, pepper
2 oz/50 g shelled pecans, toasted and roughly chopped
4 tablespoons dill, finely chopped.

1. Bring the water and oil to the boil, then remove from the heat and stir in the couscous. Season well with plenty of salt and pepper. Fork through, cover with two tea-towels, then a lid. Allow to stand for 10 minutes.
2. Fluff up the couscous with a fork and stir in the pecans and the dill. Serve at once.
NOTE: Do not freeze.

Dill and Salmon Pilaff in Filo Pastry

This is a marvellous blend of two classic dishes from totally different cuisines. First, there is the Turkish dish, Iç Pilav, which is a mixture of rice, currants, pine kernels and dill, usually served as an accompaniment to roast meats, such as leg of lamb. There is also some cinnamon in the flavouring which, perhaps surprisingly, works well with the dill. Then there is the well known Russian Koulebiaca or Coulibiac. Often described as The Tsar of Russian pies, it is a most sumptuous dish, with many different layers: rice, salmon, eggs, mushrooms and, of course, dill. It is often to be found wrapped in buttery puff pastry, although authentically it was made with an enriched brioche dough. There are endless variations on the filling; sometimes smoked as well as fresh salmon is used, or little thin pancakes are layered on to the fish, or buckwheat or milled wheat used instead of rice; or wild mushrooms as well as cultivated ones. Served with a cold sour cream, both these recipes make full use of fresh dill and so my resulting recipe is a combination of both.

The filling is a Turkish style pilaff layered into a pie tin with some smoked salmon, then topped with light, buttery filo pastry. A brioche dough or even puff pastry would be too heavy for this recipe. So filo is perfect; it looks fabulous but is very light. If you have not used filo pastry before, ensure that it is well defrosted (I ignore the packet instructions and always leave it overnight in the fridge). Have a clean tea towel at the ready: the moment you remove one sheet of the pastry (very carefully or it might tear), cover the remaining sheets with the tea towel, otherwise they will dry out and become unusable. Although I have stipulated the use of 5 to 6 sheets of filo, you might need more, or indeed less, depending on how large they are. This delicious dish can be prepared completely in the morning and kept unbaked in the fridge until evening. Do not leave it for more than 8 hours before baking, however. (serves 6)

Rice

2 oz/50 g butter
1 onion, peeled and finely chopped
2 oz/50 g currants
2 oz/50 g pine kernels
12 oz/375 g long-grain rice
¾ teaspoon cinnamon
¾ pint/450 ml chicken stock
salt, pepper
5 tablespoons dill, chopped

Filling & Pastry

1 oz/25 g butter
1 tablespoon olive oil
6 sheets filo pastry
4 oz/125 g smoked salmon slices
1 oz/25 g flaked almonds

1. First cook the rice. Heat the butter in a saucepan and add the onion. Fry for 2–3 minutes, then add the currants, pine kernels, rice and cinnamon. Stir to combine.

2. Add the stock, some salt and pepper and bring to the boil. Cover, reduce the heat and simmer until the rice is cooked and the liquid absorbed. Cook to room temperature, then stir in the dill.

3. Preheat the oven to Gas Mark 6/200°C/400°F. To assemble the pie, you must work very quickly. Melt the butter and oil together. Butter a 8½ in/22 cm deep, loose-bottomed tin very well. Line with a sheet of filo, leaving the edges to come up the sides. Brush with the butter/oil mixture. Then place another sheet of pastry, at right angles to the first, then the remaining sheets, each time brushing with the butter/oil. Each time, you should move the tin around a little, so they are positioned at different angles; the effect, once you have put in all 5 or 6 sheets, is a rather ragged-looking edge.

4. Pack half the rice mixture into the tin. Then place the smoked salmon slices on top, trying not to overlap. Season with black pepper. Continue with the remaining half of the rice, pressing down tightly. Then fold over the pastry, one corner at a time. The result will be a fairly crumpled top; do not press down with the brush or the pastry will become flattened.

5. Sprinkle over the flaked almonds, and bake in the middle of the preheated oven for 30–35 minutes, until the filo is golden. Allow it to cool for 15–20 minutes, then carefully decant and serve warm.

NOTE: Do not freeze.

Dill Pasta with Crab and Mascarpone

If you panic at the thought of making your own pasta, please read on. I make mine in the food processor (although if you prefer to do it by hand, simply mix everything together in a bowl – it takes only about double the amount of time). Then I roll it out with my pasta machine. Again, if you do not have a machine, then you can roll it out by hand, but you do need lots of room. Also, it can be difficult to achieve a uniform thickness – or rather thinness. I have used dill in this recipe, but once you get the hang of making it, you will be chopping all kinds of herbs into pasta. Ones I recommend are basil, parsley, chervil, thyme and sage. Think which flavours it would go with and then let your imagination run riot. I do, however, draw the line at those recipes advocating chocolate-flavoured pasta! Buy fresh crabmeat if at all possible, although frozen is fine. Of course, the very best is to buy live crabs and cook them yourself. Although there are those who plunge them straight into boiling water, I prefer a quick stab through the heart (which is easily located through a tiny hole between the 'purse' and eyes, on the underbelly). Then bring them to the boil in cold water and boil for a maximum of 15 minutes. Then, while you are scooping out the wonderfully sweet meat and the creamy brown meat, just remember to discard the 'dead men's fingers'; these are 6 pairs of feathery gills, which are very easy to find, so do not be put off. In this recipe, the delicate dill flavour of the pasta enhances the sweet-tasting crabmeat. Toss in some freshly chopped dill at the very end, for added colour. (serves 4)

Pasta
8½ oz/260 g strong white flour
½ teaspoon salt
2 heaped tablespoon dill, chopped
2 large eggs

Sauce
1 oz/25 g butter
12 oz/375 g crabmeat (half brown, half white)
8 oz/250 g mascarpone cheese
salt, pepper

To serve
1 tablespoon dill, freshly chopped

1. For the pasta, place the flour, salt and dill in a food processor and process briefly. Add the eggs and process until it resembles moist breadcrumbs. Using your hand, combine this into a ball, knead very briefly and chill, wrapped in clingfilm, in the fridge for half an hour.

2. Using your pasta machine, roll out to the penultimate setting and cut into tagliatelle. Boil for no more than 1 minute, then toss with the butter.

3. Add the crabmeat, mascarpone and plenty of salt and pepper. Mix well together, then reheat over a low heat for 2–3 minutes, until everything is piping hot.

4. At the very end, toss in the remaining dill, then serve in warmed bowls.

NOTE: The pasta can be frozen. Cook without defrosting, for an extra minute.

Dill Crêpes with Prawns and Gherkins

You can add many different herbs to a crêpe batter, before frying. The crêpes end up not only tasting great, but looking wonderful, all speckled with green. I particularly like dill-flavoured crêpes, but do try it with either parsley, sorrel, rocket, basil or chives. They freeze well, but it makes for easier separation if you layer them together with greaseproof paper. However, this is not necessary if you are going to eat them just after cooking. The filling is a combination of chunky prawns and gherkins (which you might find also called cornichons) and a mixture of yoghurt and crème fraîche. The appealing aspect of this dish for me is that the crêpes are served hot and the filling cold (but not straight from the fridge), so the contrast in temperature works really well. Either serve as a summer starter or as a light lunch. (serves 4)

Crêpes
4 oz/125 g plain flour, sifted
½ pint /300 ml milk
1 large egg
2 heaped tablespoons dill, chopped
salt, pepper
butter, to fry

Filling
8 oz/250 g cooked, peeled prawns (preferably tiger prawns but smaller ones will do)
6 small gherkins (or 2 large), finely chopped
½ pint/300 ml thick Greek yoghurt
2 tablespoons crème fraîche
salt, pepper
the grated zest and juice of 1 lemon

1. For the crêpes, place the first 4 ingredients in a food processor and blend until smooth.

2. Season with salt and pepper, then pour into a bowl, cover and refrigerated for at least 1 hour (although it can be kept for up to 6 hours).

3. To cook, heat a crêpe pan with a little butter (I use some kitchen paper, and rub it into the butter). Then, once it is hot enough, fry the crêpes, as normal: pour in about 1½ tablespoons, or just enough to cover the bottom of the pan, when swirled around. Once cooked on both sides, stack the crêpes on a plate, then cover with foil and keep them warm. You should get about 10 crêpes.

4. For the filling, mix together the prawns, chopped gherkins, yoghurt and crème fraiche together, then season with the salt and pepper. Stir in the lemon juice and zest at the end.

5. Place a warm crêpe on the plate and spoon some filling along the middle. Roll up and serve at once.

NOTE: The crêpes can be frozen without the filling. Layer greaseproof paper or baking parchment between each crêpe to make it easier to separate them.

Kidneys in Brioche

This is a recipe to tempt the most hardened non-kidney eaters. Since the generous addition of the dill, with its clean, sharp flavour, cuts through the richness of the kidneys, it softens their distinctive taste. The kidneys, mushrooms and dill all work very well in the warmed brioche container. Instead of 4 individual ones, you could also try serving it in a large dish, though give it longer in the oven to warm through. This makes a good starter if you are serving a fishy main course, or, depending on your constitution, a late breakfast dish. I am convinced that eating this would banish the merest suggestion of a hangover! (serves 4)

4 individual brioches
8 lamb's kidneys, trimmed
2 oz/50 g butter
8 oz/250 g mushrooms, sliced
½ oz/15 g flour
½ pint/300 ml red wine
salt, pepper
3 tablespoons dill, chopped

1. Preheat the oven to Gas Mark 3/160°C/325°F. Remove the top from the brioches and put to one side. Take out a little of the bread from the inside of the lower part, just enough to make a golf-ball sized hole.

2. Put the brioches, with their lids, on a baking tray in the oven for about 10 minutes or until crispy and hot.

3. Meanwhile prepare the kidneys. If there is still a thin, transparent skin around them, remove it. Slice them in half lengthways and cut out the central core. Heat the butter in a heavy frying pan, add the kidneys and fry for about 3 minutes on each side. Remove them with a slotted spoon and keep warm. Put the mushrooms and flour into the frying pan and stir well. Cook for 1–2 minutes, stirring constantly.

4. Add the red wine and bring to the boil. Bubble for 2–3 minutes, stirring constantly, until it has slightly thickened. Taste and season with salt and pepper.

5. Lower the heat. Using a slotted spoon, return the kidneys to the pan and add the dill. Stir, and cover with a lid. Cook for a further 4–5 minutes, until the kidneys are just cooked.

6. To serve, put one brioche on each plate, then carefully spoon a quarter of the kidney mixture into each. Do not worry if most of the sauce dribbles down the side – it looks even more appealing! Top with the lid and serve at once.

NOTE: Do not freeze.

chapter 7

fennel

I t is very important to distinguish between the herb fennel and the vegetable, which is called Florence fennel (finocchio) or bulb fennel. The latter is only one variety of fennel, which is grown particularly for its thick base. The vegetable is becoming increasingly popular in this country, although in Italy it has been used for some time, baked, steamed or in salads.

A Mediterranean herb, fennel (*Foeniculum vulgare*) is a hardy perennial which can grow up to about 5 feet tall. It is a very graceful-looking plant, with bright green feathery leaves, which is not only decorative in a garden, but also very useful. Bronze fennel is a form of fennel which has bronze, almost purplish coloured foliage; it is good for salads and garnish, because the colour is so unusual. The taste is identical to the green herb. I like to add it to mixed leaf salads, to serve with a grilled or steamed fish dish.

Because of its sweet perfume and distinct aniseed flavour, fennel has been used, over the centuries, as a digestive breath sweetener, to be chewed after meals. It was applied by Ancient Greek herbalists to help to clear vision and improve bad eyesight. Today fennel infusions are still recommended as a treatment for inflamed and sore eyes. Warm fennel tea is also given as a diuretic and mild laxative. This dates back to the Sixteenth century, when fennel decoctions were given 'to make people more lean that are too fat'. It was meant to assuage hunger and cause them 'to grow more gaunt and lank'. I wonder if the makers of diet drinks are aware of this little-known fact. It could be a whole new taste sensation – better than diet coke anyday! The essential oil of fennel has also been used – and still is – as treatment for stomach pains and painful wind. Babies are sometimes given fennel water, and adults are massaged with the essential oil to relieve indigestion or flatulence.

Fennel flowers, which have an attractive yellow colour, can be scattered over salads, seafood or vegetable dishes. The herb has always been linked with fish: it is now used in court bouillons, fennel sauces, mayonnaises and stuffings for fish. The anise taste of the herb contrasts well with the richness of oily fish; it aids the digestion of fatty foods. Fennel is often teamed up with smoked mackerel or salmon. Combined with a classic gooseberry sauce, it is the perfect accompaniment to grilled fresh mackerel or herring.

In Italy fennel is used extensively with pork: it is often made as a stuffing for suckling pigs and forms a marinade for wild boar. Chop it finely and add to veal dishes or to soups, salads, breads, cakes and scones. Also try chopping some leaves over freshly boiled new potatoes instead of mint or parsley. Add it to a dish of Jerusalem artichokes, beetroot or tomatoes. In Florence, there is a salami called Finocchiona, which is highly flavoured with fennel seeds – a very popular local speciality. Some Italian and French alcoholic drinks, such as the liqueur 'fenouillette', are flavoured with fennel. These are ideal digestives to take after a rich meal. And who knows, they might even help us shed the pounds we have just inadvertently put on!

Watercress Salad with Coconut Dressing

I happen to love watercress and am also inspired by the knowledge that it is so good for me! The dressing for this easy salad is made from coconut milk, which can be bought in tins in most supermarkets and delicatessens. It is mixed with freshly squeezed lime juice and a dash of chilli sauce. Add the chilli sauce drop by drop, tasting as you go. Different sauces vary in strength, so you do not want to make any irredeemable errors by sloshing in too much! The fennel flavour should come through loud and clear, so do take care not to overdo the chilli. Always toast the walnuts before tossing them into the salad: all nuts benefit from a minute or two under the grill or in a hot oven, to bring out the full nutty flavour. (serves 4)

Salad
6 oz/175 g watercress (prepared weight), washed
2 oz/50 g walnuts, toasted

Dressing
¼ pint/150 ml coconut milk
the juice of ½ a large lime
2 heaped tablespoons fennel, finely chopped
salt, pepper
½ teaspoons chilli sauce

1. Place the watercress and walnuts in a large salad bowl.
2. Whisk the dressing ingredients together, adding the salt, pepper and chilli sauce at the end, according to taste.
3. Just before serving, toss the dressing over the salad and serve at once. NOTE: Do not freeze.

Fennel coleslaw

There are coleslaws and coleslaws. Some, laden with far too much heavy mayonnaise and tired cabbage, do nothing for the reputation of a dish which can be so fresh, crunchy and interesting when well made. This coleslaw, which is ideal for picnics or barbecues, is made with the usual white cabbage, but also includes bulb fennel to add to the general anise flavour. The type of fennel I like to use for this is bronze fennel, as its colour is so pretty, contrasting against the creamy white dressing. If you cannot find bronze fennel, then the green variety will do very well. (serves 4–6)

Dressing
2 tablespoons crème fraîche
3 tablespoons mayonnaise
1 tablespoon balsamic vinegar
1 garlic clove, crushed
salt, pepper
2 teaspoons wholegrain mustard
3 tablespoons bronze fennel, finely chopped

Salad
1 large bulb of fennel
1 lb/500 g white cabbage
1 crispy lettuce, washed

1. Mix all the dressing ingredients together, until well blended. Taste for seasoning.
2. Shred or very finely slice the fennel bulb and the cabbage and place in a large bowl. Pour over the salad dressing and stir well, so it is all coated. (This can now be covered with clingfilm and chilled for 1–2 hours.)
3. Line a large salad bowl with leaves of crispy lettuce, then pour in the fennel coleslaw. Serve at room temperature.

NOTE: Do not freeze.

Asparagus with Fennel Mayonnaise

Dipping food into sauces and dips is not only extremely convivial, it is also great fun. There are so many Far Eastern dishes where you have a small dish of dipping soy, fish or chilli-based sauce, to dip into. In the States, there are numerous dips, which are usually based on sour cream or mayonnaise, and served with raw vegetables or potato crisps or chips. Artichokes and asparagus are two vegetables which are still deemed rather glamorous. Goodness knows why, since they are two of the messiest vegetables to eat – if you eat them with gusto (i.e. fingers)! Both can be simply steamed or boiled, then dipped into either foamy hollandaise or a luscious mayonnaise. I have selected the latter, flavoured with fennel, to form the accompanying sauce with the asparagus. When local asparagus is out of season, use globe artichokes instead, to dip into this creamy, herby mayonnaise. (serves 4 as a starter)

1–1¼ lb/500–625 g asparagus

Mayonnaise
1 egg
½ teaspoon dijon mustard
1 tablespoon freshly squeezed lemon juice
salt, pepper
4 tablespoons fennel
5 fl oz/150 ml sunflower oil
3 fl oz/90 ml extra-virgin olive oil
a squeeze of lemon juice (optional)

1. Trim the asparagus: snap off the woody ends then trim them with a knife to neaten.
2. Steam them or lay them, piled on top of each other if necessary, in a large saucepan and cook in boiling water. Timing depends completely on the thickness of the stems. After 4–5 minutes, start prodding these with a sharp knife, to test whether they are tender. They should not take more than 10 minutes. Drain them and keep them warm.
3. To make the mayonnaise, place the first five ingredients in a food processor, with the metal blade. Process for about 10 seconds, until the fennel is well chopped.
4. Very slowly indeed (drop by drop at first, then in a thin stream), add the sunflower oil through the feeder tube, while the processor is running. Then add the olive oil. You should now have a fairly thick, creamy-textured mayonnaise. Taste and check for seasoning and if you like, add a drop or two of lemon juice. Pour into a bowl.
5. To serve, give everyone a plate and let them help themselves to the hot asparagus, which they dip into the bowl of mayonnaise.

NOTE: Do not freeze.

Beetroot and Fennel Risotto

This risotto is rather unusual, not simply because of the combination of beetroot and fennel, but also because of the colour. Since there is red wine and beetroot in the recipe, it becomes the most wonderful bright pink colour. Be sure to use only cooked beetroot, not those pickled in vinegar; otherwise the taste will be overpoweringly vinegary. You can, of course, cook them yourself very easily. Either bake (at Gas Mark 6/ 200°C/400°F) or boil them for about 1–1½ hours. Once they are cool enough to handle, simply rub off the skins. Do not cut off the tops, or the juices will bleed out. Try twisting them off instead. The addition of Parmesan cheese to the risotto depends on whether you are to serve this dish as a vegetarian main course, or as an accompaniment. Served on its own, I would offer a tablespoon or so of freshly grated Parmesan cheese, but as a side-dish, I prefer it without. It goes very well with roast pork or veal or a baked whole fish such as sea bream, sea bass or red snapper. (serves 4)

1 pint/600 ml vegetable or chicken stock
3 tablespoons olive oil
1 small onion, peeled and finely chopped
2 sticks of celery, finely chopped
9 oz/275 g arborio (risotto) rice
¼ pint/150 ml red wine
6 oz/175 g cooked beetroot, cut into chunks
3 tablespoons fennel, chopped
salt, pepper

To finish
½ tablespoon extra-virgin olive oil
1 tablespoon fennel, finely chopped

1. Bring the stock to the boil, and allow it to simmer while you proceed.
2. Heat the oil in a heavy saucepan, and cook the onion and celery gently for 5 minutes.
3. Add the rice and stir. Add the red wine and bring it to the boil. Bubble for 2 minutes, then reduce the heat and gradually add the stock. Do this ladleful by ladleful, allowing each ladle of stock to be completely absorbed before adding more.
4. After 15 minutes, add the beetroot and fennel. Continue adding sufficient stock until the rice is tender. (The whole dish should take no more than 30 minutes altogether.)
5. Season to taste with salt and pepper, then stir in the oil and fennel. Cover with a lid, leave for 3–4 minutes, then serve, preferably straight from the pan.

NOTE: Do not freeze.

Stilton and Fennel Tart

I just love tarts, pies, flans and quiches. I hesitate to use the latter word, as 'quiche' seems to have gone out of fashion somewhat. That is probably because of the bastardised versions of the classic French quiche lorraine which invaded our cafés, restaurants and wine bars in the 1980s. Not all the so-called innovative variations were unqualified successes! Stilton in a pastry case, however, is – I think – more than worthy of inclusion among the all-time great tarts. For Stilton, that king of English cheeses, is transformed from a somewhat overpowering, strong cheese to a light, subtle flavour in this unusual and delicious recipe. The fennel adds not only terrific colour to the custard, but also a fresh, anise flavour, which contrasts beautifully with the buttery creaminess of the cheese. I prefer to use Colston Basset Stilton from Nottinghamshire, as its taste is undeniably superior to factory-produced processed cheese. (serves 8 as starters, 4–6 as a main meal)

Pastry
8 oz/250 g plain flour, sifted
½ teaspoons salt
4 oz/125 g unsalted butter, cubed
1 egg, beaten
½ tablespoons olive oil

Filling
4 oz/125 g Stilton cheese, cubed
4 spring onions, finely chopped
¼ pint/150 ml milk
¼ pint/150 ml double cream
2 large (size 1) eggs
3 tablespoons fennel, chopped
salt, pepper

1. For the pastry, place the flour, salt and butter in the food processor. Process until resembles breadcrumbs. Slowly add the egg and oil, through the feeder tube. Stop the machine and bring the dough together with your hands. Wrap in clingfilm and chill for at least 1 hour.

2. Then roll our the dough to fit a 9 in/23 cm metal tart tin, preferably with loose bottom. Prick all over and chill again for about 1 hour or overnight.

3. Preheat the oven to Gas Mark 6/200°C/400°F. Line the tart with foil, then fill with baking beans. Bake in the oven for 10 minutes, then remove the foil and beans. Bake for another 5 minutes, then remove.

4. Lower the oven temperature to Gas Mark 5/190°C/375°F.

5. For the filling, place the cheese, spring onions, milk, cream, eggs and fennel in the food processor or in a large bowl. Process or beat well with a whisk until smooth, then season with salt and pepper.

6. Pour into the pastry case, then bake in the oven for 25 minutes. Then turn off the heat and, with the door shut, keep the tart inside the oven for a further 15 minutes. Then remove and allow to cool. The tart is best served barely warm or at room temperature. (Neither hot nor straight from the fridge.)

NOTE: It is better not frozen.

Fennel Scones

Having been brought up on home-baking, I still love making scones. I fondly remember not only plain scones, but also those flavoured with raisins, treacle and – my favourite – cheese. These fennel scones are a variation on the savoury cheese scone theme. There is only a minor role for the cheese, as the star of the show is the fennel. You need quite a lot to flavour this amount of dough, so do not panic when you see a whole 2 tablespoons going in. They should be served warm, ideally about 15 minutes after emerging, golden brown, from the oven. Serve them with a bowl of soup at lunch, or with an afternoon cup of tea, or even with pre-dinner drinks: a far cry from dainty little canapés, but most welcome nonetheless! (makes 8–12)

6 oz/175 g self-raising flour
2 oz/50 g wholemeal self-raising flour
1 teaspoon baking powder
½ teaspoon salt
2 heaped tablespoons fennel, chopped
2 oz/50 g unsalted butter, cubed
1 oz/25 g Parmesan, freshly grated
1 egg, beaten
2–3 tablespoons milk
butter, for greasing

1. Preheat the oven to Gas Mark 7/220°C/425°F. Sift the flours and baking powder with the salt into a bowl, and stir in the fennel.

2. Rub in the butter, until the mixture resembles breadcrumbs and stir in the Parmesan.

3. Add the egg, then sufficient milk to make a soft dough, which leaves the bowl easily. (Do this with your hands, it is easier.)

4. Without overhandling the dough, roll it out, on a floured board to about ½ in/1 cm thickness. Cut out into scones using a pastry cutter.

5. Place the scones on a lightly buttered baking tray and bake in the preheated oven for about 10–12 minutes, (depending on size of cutter), until they are risen and golden brown.

6. Remove to a wire rack and cool slightly, then serve warm with unsalted butter.

NOTE: These freeze very well.

Fennel and Fish Pie

Fish pie sounds neither grand nor sophisticated, but it does have an air of old-fashioned goodness about it. Along with steamed puddings, it is possibly the most evocative comfort food. The wonderful thing about fish pies are that they so versatile. The type of fish you use can vary according to season and availability. I have suggested a mixture of cod and one of two cheaper white fish, coley or ling, but you could use whiting, haddock or even smoked fish. You can eke it out by adding prawns, or hard-boiled eggs and capers. However, the mainstay of the dish is the fennel, for its colour and flavour are simply superb with the fish. You can prepare the pie partly in advance, in fact the day before. Start at stage 2 and go as far as filling the pie dish. Then cover with clingfilm and refrigerate. The potato topping, however. must not be prepared until just before you are about to bake the pie. All you need to accompany the pie is a crisp green salad. (serves 6)

2 lb/1 kg large potatoes, peeled and left whole
2 lb/1 kg skinless fillets of cod and either coley or ling.
¾ pint/450 ml creamy milk
1½ oz/40 g fennel stalks and leaves
6 peppercorns
3 oz/75 g butter
6 oz/175 g button mushrooms, thinly sliced
1½ oz/40 g plain flour
½ pint/150 ml fish stock
the juice of ½ a lemon
salt, pepper
2 tablespoons freshly grated Parmesan cheese

1. Boil the whole potatoes for about 15 minutes, until not quite cooked. When you prod with a sharp knife, they will still feel slightly hard in the very centre. Drain.

2. Place the cod and coley or ling in a large saucepan with the milk and the stalks of the fennel. Add the peppercorns, then slowly bring it to the boil. Cover, reduce the heat and simmer for 5 minutes, or until just cooked. Drain the fish, reserving the milk. Flake the fish, in large chunks, into a large deep ovenproof dish.

3. In another saucepan, melt 2 oz/50 g of the butter, then add the mushrooms and cook for 2–3 minutes. Then add the flour and cook for a further 1 minute or so, mixing well. Gradually add the fish stock and the reserved milk, stirring all the time. Cook, stirring or whisking occasionally, for 8–10 minutes, until thickened. Meanwhile, chop the fennel leaves finely.

4. Remove the sauce from the heat and stir in the fennel leaves, the lemon juice and salt and pepper to taste. Pour it evenly over the fish.

5. Preheat the oven to Gas Mark 5/190°C/375°F.Cut the potatoes into thin slices and arrange them, overlapping slightly, on top of the sauce.

6. Melt the remaining 1 oz/25 g of butter and brush it over the top, then sprinkle over the Parmesan. Bake in the preheated oven for 40–50 minutes, until golden brown and bubbling.

NOTE: Do not freeze.

Red Mullet with Fennel and Pine Kernels

This is a variation of a classic southern French dish, where red mullet are barbecued over fennel stalks. The stalks are then doused with brandy and ignited. Once the flames have died down, the fish is eventually eaten with great gusto. Since barbecues are not possible in this country for much of the year, this is a version to suit the average Brit, not the pyromaniac of Provence! Red mullet is caught off the southern coast of Britain in summer. Out of season, either use frozen (they keep their firm flesh remarkably well, for frozen fish) or substitute small trout. If you have forgotten to ask your fishmonger to gut and scale them, this is a very easy task with such small fish. Simply run the blunt edge of your knife along the fish, from tail to head, and all the scales will come off. (They will fly everywhere, so do this over newspaper or in a large sink.) Then cut along the belly and, using your fingers, pull out the guts. Wash very thoroughly and dry well, before stuffing. (serves 4)

4 red mullet, about 10 oz/300 g each, scaled and gutted
salt
1 oz/25 g fennel stalks and leaves
3 tablespoons olive oil
1 large lime
3 oz/75 g pine kernels

1. Wash and dry the fish, then salt the insides lightly. Slash a couple of slits in each side of the fish. Tuck in as much fennel as possible into the belly cavity, then place the fish, side by side (but not touching), on an oiled grill-proof dish.

2. Squeeze over the juice of the lime, then pour over 2 tablespoons of the oil, rubbing with your hands to make sure the whole area is covered.

3. Place the fish under a preheated, hot grill and grill for about 5–6 minutes (depending on how near the grill your dish is). Then turn the fish over and grill for a further 5–6 minutes, until cooked through.

4. Meanwhile, heat the remaining 1 tablespoon oil in a frying pan and fry the pine kernels for about 3 minutes, until golden.

5. To serve, place the fish on to a serving plate, spoon over the pan juices, and top with the pine kernels.

NOTE: Do not freeze. If using frozen fish, be sure they are completely defrosted before using.

chapter 8

lovage

In a blind tasting, it would be very easy to recognise the distinctive flavour of lovage. Yet trying to describe it is more difficult. The first thing to strike you is the smell, which is very reminiscent of celery. On tasting, you become aware of a powerful savoury, lemony taste. So a flavour somewhere between citrus and celery is appropriate to describe lovage.

Lovage (*Levisticum officinale*) is very easy to grow, preferring a rich, moist soil and plenty of sunshine. It can be raised from seeds or propagated by root division. It can grow as tall as 7 or 8 feet high and is an extremely handsome plant, with dark green, polished leaves. Sadly, it is rather a neglected herb nowadays, although it has been put to both culinary and medicinal uses over the centuries. It is more popular as an ornamental plant, such is its grandeur and beauty. The greenish-yellow flowers of the lovage plant, which resemble fennel flowers, bloom in early summer and add to its attraction.

It was much used by both the Greeks and the Romans, as an antiseptic remedy, for treating intestinal troubles and jaundice. Since the fourteenth century, when lovage was introduced to English gardens, it was used for cooking, as well as for its medicinal purposes. It became a favourite salad herb for the Tudors and the Stuarts, and it was also extremely popular made into a cordial.

Any recipe in which you are lucky enough to come across lovage usually stipulates chopping only the leaves into sauces, soups or salads. However, the stems, which are hollow, are quite delicious when blanched and eaten like celery. Drop them into boiling water for 2 to 3 minutes, depending on their thickness and treat them either as celery or – and this is my favourite – asparagus. Dip them into melted butter or hollandaise sauce, or drizzle over some olive oil and top with shavings of Parmesan cheese. If you prefer lovage sweet, candy the stems like angelica.

The leaves can be used in salads, either chopped into vinaigrettes or the leaves rubbed directly into the salad bowl, as you would a garlic clove. They are good with many fish, meat or vegetable dishes. I particularly like them with smoked fish or smoked meat. Try poaching some finnan haddock or smoked haddock cutlets in a little cream or butter, which you have flavoured with some chopped lovage leaves. It transforms a very simple dish into something quite sophisticated. Or add them to scones or breads, as you might add a teaspoon of celery salt. Soups benefit from the addition of not only the leaves, but also the stalks. Be circumspect in you measurements, however, for the flavour of lovage is deceptively strong. Unless it is matching another bold flavour, it tends to dominate.

Lovage is one of the most interesting old-fashioned herbs. Once you start experimenting with it, you will appreciate how very versatile this beautiful plant is. Add with caution at first, then become more adventurous as you get to know and love this aptly named herb.

Lovage and Saffron Kedgeree

This is the most ideal kedgeree, as it can be made the night before and heated up as you fumble around in the kitchen for that first essential morning cup of tea. I have tried using other types of fish – even kippers – but I always come back to smoked haddock. It seems to make the most authentic dish. This recipe is, of course, slightly different form the classic. There is saffron, for a start, which not only colours the dish, but also imparts a wonderfully spicy flavour. I like to roast the strands of saffron before infusing, as this emphasises the flavour. The lovage adds that beautiful celery-like taste, which goes well with the fish and the eggs. If you are having guests for a weekend, producing kedgeree on the Sunday morning is a lot less work than standing frying sausages, bacon and eggs. Believe me, it will go down a treat. (serves 4–6)

6 oz/175 g Basmati rice	the juice of 1 lemon
salt	¼ teaspoon cayenne pepper
¼ teaspoon saffron threads	1 heaped tablespoon lovage leaves,
¼ pint/150 ml double cream	chopped
3 hard-boiled eggs, quartered	2 oz/50 g butter, melted
1 lb/500 g smoked haddock fillets,	
cooked and flaked into chunks	

1. Cook the rice in salted water until light and fluffy, then drain well.
2. Preheat the oven to Gas Mark 4/180°C/350°F. Place the saffron threads on a dish in the preheated oven for 10 minutes.
3. Pour the cream into a small saucepan and add the saffron. Warm it slowly and remove form the heat just before it comes to the boil. Cover and leave to infuse for 10 minutes.
4. Mix the rice gently with the saffron cream, the eggs and the fish. Add the lemon juice, cayenne and lovage, then stir in the melted butter, and season to taste with salt.
5. Tip into an ovenproof dish, cover, and either place in a preheated oven (Gas Mark 4/180°C/350°F) now, or chill overnight in the fridge and reheat the next day. It will need about 25 minutes if heated at once, or 30–35 minutes if chilled overnight.

NOTE: Do not freeze.

Tuna Carpaccio with Lovage Salsa

The idea of serving raw tuna might not appeal to everyone, but think of the popular and beautifully presented Japanese sashimi, slivers of raw fish – halibut, salmon and tuna, served with a simple sauce, such as the pungent Japanese horseradish, wasabi. The important thing to remember about either sashimi or carpaccio, which is the Italian version, using raw, sliced beef served with truffle oil and Parmesan, is that the fish – or meat – should be as fresh as possible. So, only make this dish if you know your fishmonger well! Supermarket pre-packs will definitely not do. You also need incredibly sharp knives to cut the fish as thinly as possible. A tip for easy cutting (and this applies to beef too) is to pop the piece of fish into the freezer for an hour or so. It is much easier to cut after it has firmed up in the freezer. It is, of course, essential that the fish you use has never been previously frozen. The tuna (usually blue-fin tuna, from the Mediterranean, at my fishmonger's) should be fillet or loin of tuna, which is a dark red colour and very lean. Cut it as thinly as possible. Eat and enjoy this marvellous combination. (serves 4–6 as a starter)

6 oz/175 g fresh tuna fillet

Salsa
1 thick slice of bread, soaked in 2
   tablespoons of milk
1 oz/25 g lovage leaves
1 tablespoon capers
2 garlic cloves, peeled and chopped

3 anchovy fillets
juice of ½ a lemon
pepper
about 2 tablespoons olive oil

To serve
thin slices of rye bread

1. Using a very sharp knife, cut very thin slices of the tuna (or ask your fishmonger do do this for you) and arrange on a plate. Decorate with lovage leaves and slivers of lemon, if you like.

2. Place all the salsa ingredients except the oil into the food processor (the bread will have soaked up all the milk), Process for a few seconds, then slowly add sufficient oil to make a fairly thick sauce. Taste and add some pepper accordingly. (You will probably not need to add salt, as the anchovies are salty.)

3. To serve, place the salsa in a bowl and allow your guests to assemble the rye bread spread with lovage salsa, then the tuna on top.

NOTE: Do not freeze.

Arbroath Smokie and Lovage Soup

This soup has the most wonderfully creamy texture. The idea for it comes for Margaret Horn, who cooks in the But'n Ben Restaurant, at Auchmithie. I have added lovage for extra flavour. A bowl of this soup and some warm soda bread with good butter is, to my mind, the most perfect meal on a winter's day. (serves 6)

1 pair of Arbroath smokies
2 oz/50 g lovage stalks and leaves, plus
   1 heaped tablespoon lovage leaves
1 medium onion, peeled and chopped

1 leek, cleaned and sliced
1 lb/500 g potatoes, peeled and cubed
salt, pepper
¼ pint/150 ml double cream

1. Gently heat the smokies (either in a low oven for 10 minutes or in a microwave for 2 minutes), then remove the flesh, taking care to avoid the tiny creamy-coloured bones.

2. Reserve the flesh, and place all the rest – skin and bones – in a large saucepan. Add the lovage stalks and leaves, then cover with 2 pints/1.2 litres of cold water. Bring to the boil, then cover and simmer for 25 minutes, stirring twice.

3. Strain into a clean saucepan, then add the onion, leek and potatoes. Bring to the boil and simmer for about 20 minutes, or until the vegetables are tender.

4. Liquidise this with the reserved flesh, and 1 tablespoon lovage leaves, either in a blender or liquidiser (if you use a food processor, it might not eliminate any rogue fish bones).

5. Taste, then season (it will probably need only pepper, as the fish is fairly salty). Pour back in to the pan, then add the cream. Reheat gently, without boiling, until piping hot. Serve in warmed bowls. (You can drizzle some extra cream over the top if you like.)

NOTE: Do not freeze.

Grilled Pepper Soup

For this colourful soup you can use either red (my preference), orange or yellow peppers – or a combination of the three. The flavour of the soup is enhanced by grilling the peppers first. (serves 4)

1 lb/500 g (red) peppers, cut, deseeded and quartered	1 tablespoon tomato purée
1 tablespoon olive oil	1¼ pint/750 ml chicken stock
1 onion, peeled and chopped	salt, pepper
2 garlic cloves, peeled and chopped	<u>To serve</u>
2 tablespoons lovage leaves, chopped	a small carton of sour cream
	a few lovage leaves, finely chopped

1. Place the peppers, on a sheet of foil, under a hot grill. Grill until they are charred and blackened. Remove, wrap in the foil and leave for about 15 minutes, or until cool enough to handle. Remove the skins, and chop the flesh.

2. Heat the oil, then fry the onion and garlic gently for 5 minutes. Add the peppers and fry for a further 3 minutes. Then add the lovage, tomato purée and stock. Bring to the boil, cover and simmer for about 10 minutes.

3. Blend or liquidise, then season to taste and reheat if necessary.

4. Serve with a dollop of sour cream, topped with the chopped lovage leaves. NOTE: Freezes well.

Bacon and Egg Salad

Bacon and egg in a salad might sound rather a curious combination, but the result is delicious. It is essential to poach the eggs the 'real' way, in a pan of simmering water, using two spoons to shape them. The yolk from the egg adds to the flavour of the dressing. I like to serve this for lunch with bread to dunk in the dressing. It can either be made in one large salad bowl or 4 individual bowls. (serves 4)

mixed green salad leaves, (eg cos, webb)	<u>Dressing</u>
4 free-range eggs	3 tablespoons olive oil
salt	1 tablespoon hazelnut oil
vinegar	1 tablespoon white wine vinegar
3 tablespoons olive oil	2 tablespoons lovage leaves, very finely
2 thick slices bread, cubed	chopped
4 thick rashers smoked back bacon, cut into cubes	salt, pepper

1. Place the washed salad leaves into a bowl.

2. Poach the eggs in simmering water, to which a pinch of salt and a drop or two of vinegar has been added. Cook them for 3–4 minutes, the yolks should be still runny. Carefully remove them with a slotted spoon and drain on paper towels.

3. Heat 2 tablespoons of the oil in a frying pan and fry the bread until crispy. Remove, and add the remaining oil, fry the bacon until crisp and golden.

4. Shake all the dressing ingredients together in a screw-top jar and pour over the salad leaves. Toss well. Add the croutons and bacon and toss again. Place the poached eggs on top, grind over some black pepper and serve at once. NOTE: Do not freeze.

Smoked Haddock and Lovage Tart

The flavours of smoked fish and lovage go so well together that I could not resists putting them into a tart. For the pastry, I have added a little polenta, which not only gives it an extra-short texture, but also makes it a brilliant yellow colour. If, however, you cannot find polenta, then just use your favourite savoury shortcrust pastry recipe. This tart should be served warm or at room temperature, never piping hot or straight from the fridge. It makes a delightful supper or lunch dish, with a simple tossed salad or some steamed green vegetables such as broccoli or green beans. (serves 4–6)

Pastry
6 oz/175 g plain flour, sifted
2 oz/50 g fine polenta
½ teaspoon salt
4 oz/125 g unsalted butter, cubed
1 egg combined with 1 tablespoon olive oil

Filling
12 oz/375 g smoked haddock
¼ pint/150 ml creamy milk
¼ pint/150 ml double cream
3 eggs
2 tablespoons finely chopped lovage
salt, pepper

1. For the pastry, place the flour, polenta, salt and butter in a food processor. Process briefly, then add the egg and oil combination and process for a few seconds. Bring together with your hands, wrap in clingfilm and chill for 30 minutes.

2. Roll out to fit a 9 in/23 cm metal tart tin. It is rather a crumbly pastry: do not worry, just patch it together if necessary. Prick all over with a fork, then chill for another 30 minutes.

3. Preheat the oven to Gas Mark 5/190°C/375°F. Bake the pie case blind, lined with foil and baking beans, for 15 minutes. Remove the foil and beans and cook for a further 5 minutes. Remove and cool slightly.

4. Meanwhile poach the fish in the milk for about 5 minutes until just cooked. Drain, reserving the liquid. Flake the fish and place in the cooled pastry case.

5. Whisk the cream and eggs into the reserved liquid. Add the lovage, and season to taste. Pour this over the fish and return to the oven to cook for about 30 minutes, or until the filling is just set. Allow to cook for at least 20 minutes before serving. NOTE: Do not freeze.

Gammon with Cream and Lovage Sauce

Gammon steaks are to my mind rather a cliché, especially when served with a bright yellow pineapple slice on top, but they are in fact very tasty and also very versatile. Accompanied by this creamy lovage sauce, they are a real treat. I hesitate to suggest serving them with tinned sweetcorn, but they are actually rather good with corn. Why not try some baby corn, stirfried with mange-tout or fine green beans, and perhaps a few sauté potatoes. Sheer bliss! (serves 4)

4 tablespoons white wine vinegar	¼ pint/150 ml dry white wine
2 shallots, peeled and chopped	2 tablespoons crème fraîche
2–3 lovage stalks, torn in half	1 heaped tablespoon of lovage leaves, chopped
6 fl oz/175 ml chicken stock	salt, pepper
1 oz/25 g butter	4 unsmoked gammon steaks
1 oz/25 g plain flour	1 oz/25 g unsalted butter

1. For the sauce, place the vinegar, shallots and lovage stalks (reserve the leaves) into a pan. Bring to the boil and simmer for a couple of minutes, until there is only about 1 tablespoon of the liquid left. Strain into the stock, pressing down on the shallots and lovage in the sieve, to extract the flavour.

2. In a heavy pan, melt the butter, then add the flour. Stir to make a roux, then cook for about 3 minutes. Gradually add the flavoured stock, then the wine. Stirring or whisking, cook for about 10 minutes, until you have a smooth sauce. Then add the crème fraîche, lovage leaves and salt and pepper to taste.

3. Meanwhile, fry the gammon steaks in the unsalted butter for 3–4 minutes on each side.

4. Serve at once with some sauce poured over.

NOTE: Do not freeze.

Chicken Breasts with Stilton and Lovage

The strong flavour of Stilton cheese is often matched with celery: I have tasted excellent soups and tarts with this combination. So in this recipe I have combined this marvellous blue cheese with lovage leaves in a simple stuffing for chicken. The stuffing is in fact pushed in between the skin and the flesh of the chicken, in order to keep the breast moist, as it has a tendency to dry out. Be sure, therefore, not to overcook. The best way to test (since weight is not really the only guide – thickness makes a difference too) is to pierce the thickest part of the breast with a sharp knife; if the juices run clear, it is ready. If there is a hint of pink, then return the chicken to the oven and try in another couple of minutes. (serves 4)

2 oz/50 g Stilton, softened	freshly ground pepper
3 oz/75 g cream cheese, softened	4 boneless chicken breasts,
1 teaspoon lemon juice	with skins on
2 tablespoons lovage leaves, finely chopped	1 tablespoon olive oil.

1. Preheat the oven to Gas Mark 7/220°C/425°F. Mix the Stilton, cream cheese, lemon juice and lovage together. Season with pepper.

2. Carefully slide your finger between the skin and the flesh of the chicken breast, so that you have a pocket; do not detach the skin completely. Using your fingers, push the Stilton mixture into the pocket and smear over the flesh. Gently pat the skin over the filling again.

3. Place the chicken on an oiled ovenproof dish, brush with oil and bake in the middle of the preheated oven for about 16–18 minutes, depending on size. You can either serve them as they are, or allow them to rest for 2–3 minutes, then, using a very sharp knife, cut into 3 or 4 thick slices, and, with a fish slice, carefully remove them to warmed serving plates.

NOTE: Do not freeze.

chapter 9

marjoram

Sweet, or 'knotted' marjoram (*Origanum majorana*) is one of the three main species of marjoram. The other two are oregano (*Origanum vulgare*), subject of Chapter 11; and pot marjoram (*Origanum onites*). The latter, also called French marjoram, has a slightly bitter flavour and is less delicate than sweet marjoram and therefore goes well in boldly-flavoured dishes; those redolent of onion, garlic and red wine. All are natives of Southern Europe.

However, it is sweet marjoram which is most likely to be found in gardens and kitchens in this country. Whereas pot marjoram is a hardy perennial, sweet marjoram is treated in Britain as a half-hardy annual. It can be grown from seed or propagated from cuttings in the early summer and can grow to about 12 inches tall. It is also sometimes grown as a pot plant in a cool greenhouse. Outside, marjoram thrives in a light rich soil and a sunny, sheltered position.

The leaves of the herb are greyish-green in colour and soft in texture. Its flowers range in colour from pink to deep purple, and can be tossed over salads, poultry dishes or pizzas. The taste is spicy and scented. Used by both Greeks and Romans in cooking and in perfumes, it was later to be found in Tudor England growing in ornamental herb gardens. It was also made into 'sweet bags' and 'sweet powders', which were strewn in chambers, to combat foul odours and sweeten the air in public places. Marjoram teas have soothing properties and are recommended to calm nerves and encourage deep sleep. It was also employed in the brewing of ale, long before the introduction of hops, as a preservative as well as a flavouring.

For culinary use, marjoram is one of the most versatile herbs because of its delicately spicy flavour and its ability to blend well with other herbs. It is related to thyme, therefore the two mix well, but is far sweeter. Combine it also with oregano and, in moderation, with parsley, sage or basil. It is used nowadays in most European countries and places like Australia and America where many recipes have a European provenance but is hardly ever used in the Far East.

Since its flavour is rather more delicate than either thyme and oregano, both of which stand up well to long, slow cooking techniques, marjoram is usually added towards the end of cooking to ensure its perfume is not lost. I often add some at the initial stage of cooking, then, prior to serving, stir in some more to reinforce the flavour. The same idea goes for meatloaves, which are superb with fresh marjoram: add some to the meatloaf mix, and also to a lightly cooked sauce with which it is served. Marjoram is successful in dishes which require very little actual cooking, such as omelettes, or with pasta and also excellent in stuffings, sausages and rice dishes: try stirring some marjoram into a rice stuffing for baked green peppers. It is also good when used raw, torn over tomato salads, or scattered over freshly grilled sardines or steak, which are then dressed simply with lemon juice and olive oil.

Although marjoram is one of the herbs which does dry well, in the winter months I would always opt for fresh marjoram, imported from one of the hot Mediterranean countries, rather than resort to using dried. Fresh herbs are always – without exception – vastly superior!

Chicken Liver Paté with Marjoram

This is a classic dish which never fails to please. Its flavour is always pronounced and, depending on which herbs or other ingredients are added, it can be aromatic and creamy. The marjoram lifts the whole taste: adding a subtle sweetness to the chicken livers. I like to add whisky, for extra punch, but brandy will do just as well. If you prefer a creamier texture, you can add a tablespoon of double cream as you blend it. The method described here results in a slightly rough-textured paté, but if you prefer a very smooth paté, then do sieve it before chilling. This paté should be allowed to 'develop' for about 24 hours, then served at room temperature, with hot brown toast, or crusty granary bread. (serves 6–8)

2 oz/50 g butter	8 oz/250 g chicken livers, trimmed
3 oz/75 g back bacon, chopped	2 tablespoons marjoram, chopped
(I prefer unsmoked for this)	salt, pepper
1 medium onion, peeled and chopped	1 tablespoon whisky
2 garlic cloves, peeled and chopped	

1. Heat the butter, then add the bacon, onion and garlic and gently fry for about 10 minutes, until the vegetables are softened.
2. Increase the heat, add the livers and fry for about 3 minutes, until they are browned on the outside and still pink inside.
3. Turn off the heat, then stir in the marjoram, and salt and pepper. Add the whisky, then tip everything into the food processor and purée until well-blended. Taste for seasoning: you will need quite a lot of salt and pepper.
5. Pour into a dish, leave to cool, then cover with clingfilm and refrigerate for 24 hours. Serve at room temperature, with plenty of hot toast, or fresh bread.

NOTE: This paté freezes very well. Defrost thoroughly before serving.

Aubergine Stew with Feta and Marjoram

This vegetable stew, along the same lines as ratatouille, is full of wonderful flavours and is fairly substantial. The main ingredients are aubergine, onion and celery, while the tomatoes and red wine provide extra flavour. Once it is cooked to a thick consistency, it is then topped with the most colourful and tasty mixture of cheese and marjoram. The salty Feta cheese (try to use real Greek Feta, as its texture and flavour are better) blends well with the sweet aromatic marjoram. It should be sprinkled over the stew just before serving – not stirred in. The contrast of the uncooked herb and cheese with the cooked stew is more striking then. This is a wonderfully hearty dish for either lunch or supper; it will please vegetarians and carnivores alike. (serves 4)

2 aubergines, unpeeled, cut into dice	1 x 13 oz/400 g tin of chopped
salt	tomatoes
3 tablespoons olive oil	¼ pint/150 ml red wine
1 onion, peeled and chopped	2 tablespoons tomato purée
1 stick of celery, chopped	pepper

Topping
3 tablespoons marjoram, chopped
3 oz/75 g Feta cheese, grated or crumbled

1. First salt the aubergines. Place them on a plate and grind over a generous amount of salt. Leave for about 30 minutes, then rinse them under cold water. Pat the aubergines dry.

2. Heat the oil in a large saucepan and gently fry the onion and celery for about 5 minutes. Add the aubergines and fry for a further 5 minutes, stirring regularly. Stir in the tin of tomatoes and their juices, the wine, tomato purée and salt and pepper. Bring to the boil, then reduce the heat, cover with a lid and simmer for about 25 minutes.

5. Meanwhile, combine the Feta cheese and the chopped marjoram.

6. Taste the aubergine stew, season accordingly,. Serve at once with the marjoram and Feta topping sprinkled over the top. NOTE: Do not freeze.

Pissaladière

This Provençal tart is usually made with a bread dough base, which makes it very similar to the Italian pizza. I prefer a rather lighter base, however, made from a crisp shortcrust pastry, with some fresh marjoram chopped in. Although the classic herb used in Provence is basil, I like the contrasting sweetness of the marjoram, with the salty anchovies and olives. If the season is right, then do strew some marjoram flowers over the top of the tart just before serving. Accompany this with a simple tomato salad. (serves 4)

Pastry	Topping
2 tablespoons marjoram	3½ tablespoons olive oil
8 oz/250 g plain flour, sifted	1 onion, peeled and chopped
½ teaspoon salt	2 garlic cloves, peeled and chopped
4 oz/125 g unsalted butter, cubed	13 oz/400 g tin of chopped tomatoes
1 egg yolk	2 tablespoons red wine
1½ tablespoons cold water	1 tablespoon marjoram, chopped
	salt, pepper
	2 oz/50 g tin of anchovy fillets, drained
	10–12 black olives, stoned

1. For the pastry, place the first four ingredients in a food processor and process until it resembles breadcrumbs. Then mix the egg yolk with the water and slowly add to the processor. This should be just enough liquid for the dough to combine into a ball, when brought together with your hands. (If not, add another few drops of water.) Wrap the dough in clingfilm and chill for half an hour. Then roll out, to fit a shallow 9 in/23 cm tart tin with a removable base. Prick all over with a fork and refrigerate for 1 hour.

2. Meanwhile, start the topping. Heat 3 tablespoons of the oil in a saucepan and gently fry the onion and garlic for about 10 minutes. Add the tin of tomatoes with the juice and the red wine. Cook over a medium heat, uncovered, for about 15–20 minutes, or until it has thickened slightly. Then remove from the heat, add the marjoram, salt and pepper and allow to cool.

3. Preheat the oven to Gas Mark 6/200°C/400°F. Bake the pastry case blind with foil and baking beans for 10 minutes. Remove the foil and beans and cook for a further 5 minutes.

4. Cool the pastry case for 10–15 minutes, then fill with the tomato sauce. Top with the anchovy fillets and black olives in a lattice or criss-cross pattern.

6. Bake in the oven for about 20 minutes, then remove and drizzle over the remaining ½ tablespoon olive oil. Serve warm. NOTE: The pastry case can be frozen unbaked for 2 weeks. Bake without defrosting.

Roast Grouse with Blackcurrants & Marjoram

Grouse is one of the most strongly-flavoured game birds. For that reason, I like to serve it with seasonal soft fruits, such as blackcurrants (although brambles and raspberries will also do), and an aromatic, yet not overpowering herb, such as marjoram. Thyme is the classic accompaniment to grouse, for there is wild thyme growing in Scotland. Indeed, you could substitute thyme for the marjoram, for a change. But I am sure once you have tried this dish, you will agree the sweet, almost spicy flavour of marjoram goes very well indeed with the famous grouse of the northern moors! I like to accompany this dish with some skirlie, which is oatmeal and onions, fried in dripping (I prefer using a mixture of butter and olive oil). You could also serve it with fried breadcrumbs, or a slice of fried bread. Some seasonal vegetables are all you need to accompany the dish and perhaps a wee dram, just to help the bird down! (serves 2)

2 young grouse, cleaned and ready for the oven
2 oz/50 g butter, softened
3 oz/75 g blackcurrants, cleaned
2 tablespoons marjoram, chopped
salt, pepper
4 rashers of streaky bacon
salt, pepper
¼ pint/150 ml red wine
1 heaped teaspoon blackcurrant or redcurrant jelly

1. Preheat the oven to Gas Mark 7/220°C/425°F. Make sure the insides of the grouse are clean by washing them, then drying thoroughly.
2. Mix together the softened butter, blackcurrants and marjoram, then season with salt and pepper.
3. Carefully divide the stuffing between the birds, spooning half inside each bird.
4. Cover the breast of each grouse with 2 rashers of bacon, then place them in a lightly oiled dish.
5. Pour over the red wine. Then place in a preheated oven for 15–20 minutes, depending on the size of your birds. (20 minutes is the absolute maximum, at this high temperature.)
6. Then, using a slotted spoon, remove the grouse to a carving board and cover with foil. Allow them to rest for at least 10 minutes, before serving.
7. Place the roasting tin directly on the heat and bubble to reduce the liquid. Add the jelly and stir well to mix. Season to taste with salt and pepper and serve with the grouse on warmed plates.

NOTE: Do not freeze.

Venison with Chocolate

The combination of chocolate with game is not unusual. It is used in many Italian, Spanish and Mexican recipes. The intention is to add a deep, rich colour and flavour. Use the most bitter chocolate you can find. I like to use one with about 70 per cent cocoa solids. The marjoram enhances the sweetness of the chocolate, and both contrast well with the boldly-flavoured venison. Serve this with pappardelle (long, flat noodles) tossed in olive oil; or with hot polenta, with plenty of melted butter stirred in. (serves 4)

3 tablespoons olive oil	¼ pint/150 ml venison or beef stock
1 onion, peeled and chopped	2–3 tablespoons red wine
1 large garlic clove, peeled and chopped	1 oz/25 g bitter chocolate
1 leek, cleaned, chopped	2 tablespoons marjoram, chopped
1 lb/500 g casserole venison (I like to	salt, pepper
use shoulder), cubed	½–1 tablespoon balsamic vinegar

1. Preheat the oven to Gas Mark 3/160°C/325°F. Heat half the oil in a heavy ovenproof dish. Gently fry the onion, garlic and leek for about 10 minutes, then remove with a slotted spoon.
2. Heat the remaining oil, then brown the venison cubes all over, for a few minutes. Add the stock, wine, chocolate and marjoram. Bring to the boil, then season with salt and pepper. Cover tightly with a lid, then place in a preheated oven for 1¼–1½ hours. Stir every 30 minutes, until the meat is done. (Add another tablespoon wine if it looks dry.)
4. Taste and add enough vinegar to balance the sweetness of the sauce. (I like the full tablespoon, but you may prefer less.) Season again, with salt and pepper, and serve, piping hot.

NOTE: This dish freezes well. Defrost and reheat in a medium oven for 30–40 minutes.

Meatloaf with Red Pepper Sauce

Meatloaf recipes can be like gold dust. Each family seems to have their own, very special secret one, which is only rarely given out. My recipe is based on one I used to enjoy very often as a child at my friend Isabelle's house. Her mother made a delicious meatloaf, which was eaten warm one day, then grilled and eaten hot the next, or cut into thick slices and eaten cold, with salad or in sandwiches. The changes I have made are firstly, the addition of the marjoram – a herb which was made for meatloaves as well as rissoles, meatballs and sausages. Also, I like to serve it with a red pepper sauce, which has some extra marjoram chopped in at the end, so the cooked herb contrasts with the uncooked one in the accompanying sauce. You could alternatively serve it with a fresh tomato sauce. (serves 6)

Meatloaf	Sauce
1 lb/500 g lean minced beef	2 red peppers, quartered and deseeded
8 oz/250 g lean minced pork	5 tablespoons olive oil
3 oz/75 g fresh breadcrumbs	2 garlic cloves, peeled and chopped
1 egg	1 tablespoon marjoram, chopped
1 onion, peeled and finely chopped	salt, pepper
1 tablespoon Worcestershire sauce	
2 tablespoons marjoram, chopped	
salt, pepper	
butter, for smearing	

1. Preheat the oven to Gas Mark 2/150°C/300°F. Mix together all the meatloaf ingredients in a bowl, then season generously with salt and pepper.

2. Spoon the mixture into a buttered 2 lb/1 kg loaf tin, pressing down very well. Cover loosely with foil, place in the preheated oven and cook for about 1¾–2 hours. Then remove and allow to cool for at least 30 minutes before turning out.

3. For the sauce, place the peppers on foil and grill until blackened and charred. Then wrap them in the foil, to steam them. After about 20 minutes, or whenever they are cool enough to handle, peel away the skin, and chop them into dice.

4. Heat the oil in a saucepan and gently fry the garlic for a few minutes. Add the diced peppers and cook them for about 5 minutes, then remove from the heat and add the marjoram and salt and pepper. Tip into a food processor and process until well blended. (If you want the texture to be smooth, you might need to add more oil.) Taste, and season again if necessary. Serve warm or cold, with slices of meatloaf (which can also be warm or cold).

NOTE: The meatloaf freezes well. Defrost and reheat in a low oven for 20–30 minutes.

Barley and Mushroom with Marjoram

This is a variation on risotto, but made with pearl barley instead of arborio rice. I love the texture of the barley in the finished dish, as it is nutty and has a good bite to it. Barley is usually associated with soups, especially Scotch Broth. But, in fact, it is also excellent as a stuffing or as a substantial dish in itself – ideal for vegetarians. For carnivores, you could add some slivers of crispy fried chicken or turkey livers or some pieces of grilled smoked bacon, just before serving. The mushrooms should be wild: buy them, if you are feeling extravagant, or simply collect your own. If they are out of season and you have some dried wild mushrooms, substitute about 2 oz/50 g dried ones for the 12 oz/375 g of fresh ones – the flavour of dried mushrooms is far more intense. Soak them for at least 30 minutes (or according to packet instructions) in either warm water, wine or stock, then add them with their soaking liquid to the barley. Although this is better served warm, it will stand quite happily, with the lid on, once you have fluffed the grains up, for up to 1 hour. If this is to be served as a main course, I like to offer a bowl of freshly grated Parmesan cheese to sprinkle over the top. (serves 4)

2 oz/50 g butter	7 oz/200 g pearl barley, rinsed
2 garlic cloves, pealed and chopped	2 tablespoons marjoram, chopped
1 onion, peeled and chopped	salt, pepper
2 sticks celery, chopped	½ pint/300 ml hot vegetable or
12 oz/375 g mixed mushrooms, chopped	chicken stock

1 Preheat the oven to Gas Mark 3/160°C/325°F. Melt the butter in an ovenproof saucepan, then gently fry the garlic, onion and celery, for about 10 minutes.

2. Add the mushrooms, and cook for about 3 minutes.

3. Add the barley and stir well, to ensure it is all coated with butter. Then add 1 tablespoon of the marjoram and salt and pepper. Pour in the hot stock, bring to the boil, then cover with a lid and place in the oven for 35–40 minutes, until the liquid is absorbed.

4. Remove from the oven, add the remaining tablespoon of marjoram, season to taste and fluff up with a fork. Serve warm.

NOTE: Do not freeze.

chapter 10

mint

Under the generic name 'Mentha' – mint – are a huge variety of mints, with different shaped leaves, different tastes and textures. The herb has an interesting mythological origin: Menthe was a nymph, who was turned into the plant we now know so well by the jealous goddess Proserpine, when she discovered her husband Pluto's love for Menthe. Mint was abundantly used by the Ancient Greeks, and the Romans.

In the Middle Ages, it was used to whiten teeth, which was probably the origin of mint as a flavouring for toothpastes. It was also used as an effective hair-wash, to aid digestive disorders and stimulate lost appetites. Mint preparations are still highly recommended as mouth washes or as gargles for sore throats.

Among wild mints, water mint (*Mentha aquatica*) is most common. It grows abundantly in ditches, streams and swamps. Its flavour is rather too muddy and rank to be used for cooking. Corn mint (*Mentha arvensis*), another common wild mint, is found on arable land and in hedges. It is seldom used in cooking. The round-leaved varieties of mint (*Mentha rotundifolia*) can also be found in the wild. Apple mint, pineapple mint and Bowles mints are the best-known: all are excellent for cooking. They have soft, downy leaves and a distinctive minty flavour. Finally, pennyroyal (*Mentha pulegium*) is found wild in the South and West of England. It looks quite unlike other mints: it is a prostrate creeper, seldom used in the kitchen. In seafaring days, pennyroyal was taken in pots on the ships, so that sailors could purify their casks of stale drinking water.

As for cultivated mints, the most common is, of course, spearmint (*Mentha spicata*). Spearmint and parsley are the two herbs most likely to be found in gardens. It is important, however, to isolate spearmint, so, either grow at least 12 inches away from other plants, or in individual terracotta containers. Serve spearmint with lamb in a traditional mint sauce, which was, in fact, introduced by the Romans. Also use it with potatoes, peas, tomatoes, avocado or salmon. Add it to fruit salads and use in desserts with chocolate, apples or ginger. On hot summer days, the other essential use for mint is in a long, cool fruit cup, or drinks such as Pimms or mint juleps.

Another good cooking mint is ginger mint (*Mentha gentilis*), which has golden variegated leaves and subtle ginger taste. Eau de Cologne mint (*Mentha citrata*) has attractive bronze-purple tinged leaves, which make it useful decoratively. As it tastes slightly of lemon or orange, it combines well in fresh orange jellies or in lemon or orange based drinks. Peppermint (*Mentha piperita*) – the main cultivated varieties being white peppermint, (with green stems) and black peppermint, (with dark stems) – has a very strong flavour. Sorbets made from white peppermint are wonderfully refreshing. Peppermint creams, made from peppermint oil, if made well, can be delicious (especially if coated in best couverture chocolate).

Seafood and Mint Salad

There are Thai overtones in this unusual seafood salad. To be truly authentic, of course, there should also be some lemongrass, fresh chilli, perhaps some fresh coriander and ginger. But the principle of this salad is the combination of seafood with mint - which is very good indeed. (serves 4)

Salad
crisp salad leaves (such as cos,
   little gem, pak choy), washed
4–6 spring onions, sliced
4 tablespoons mint leaves, chopped
12 oz/375 g fresh crabmeat (half
   white, half brown)
8–12 large, cooked prawns, peeled
8 oz/250 g mushrooms (preferably
   shiitake), sliced and cooked in
   2 tablespoons olive oil for 5 minutes

Dressing
3½ oz/100 g coconut cream (about
   half a packet)
juice of 2 limes
2 tablespoons nam pla (Thai fish sauce)
2 garlic cloves, peeled and crushed
¼ teaspoon chilli sauce
1 tablespoon sunflower oil
pepper

1. For the salad, place the leaves in a large salad bowl. Using your hands, mix through the spring onions and mint leaves. With 2 salad servers mix in the crabmeat, prawns and mushrooms shortly before adding the dressing.

2. For the dressing, melt down the coconut cream with the lime juice over a very low heat. Then remove and add the remaining ingredients, stirring or whisking well to combine. Taste and see whether you need more chilli sauce (different brands vary in strength) or pepper.

3. Toss the dressing over the salad and combine well, then serve at once. NOTE: Do not freeze.

Salmon with a Mint Crust

There is a wonderful contrast of textures in this dish. The crust is crunchy and crisp, and the fish is soft and succulent. There is also a glorious colour difference – the bright pink salmon and the golden-brown and green crust. The mint mixture will keep in a screw-top jar, for several weeks in the fridge. (serves 4)

Mint crust
1 oz/25 g mint leaves
2 garlic cloves, peeled and crushed
2 oz/50 g shelled walnuts
1 oz/25 g Parmesan, freshly grated
1 tablespoon freshly squeezed lemon
   juice

3–4 tablespoons extra-virgin olive oil
salt, pepper
1½ oz/40 g fresh brown breadcrumbs

Salmon
4 salmon steaks or fillets
olive oil

1. For the crust, place the mint leaves in a food processor with the next 4 ingredients and chop. Then slowly add sufficient oil to form a thick paste. Taste and add salt and pepper. Spoon into a bowl. Shortly before cooking, mix in the breadcrumbs and stir well.

2. Rub a little oil over the salmon and lay on a foil-lined grill tray. Place under a medium-hot grill. Cook for about 4–5 minutes, then remove. Turn the fish over and spread the crust on top of each piece of fish. Return to the grill for 3–4 minutes, until the fish is just cooked. Serve at once. NOTE: The mint mixture can be frozen, before the breadcrumbs are added.

Lamb Chops with Olive and Mint Compôte

The compôte should be made at least an hour in advance, so that the flavours can blend together. Use red onions for this as other onions will be too harsh. Serve with some steamed couscous or pilaff rice. (serves 4)

¼ pint/150 ml red wine	1 tablespoon lemon juice
2 garlic cloves, peeled and crushed	4 tablespoons mint leaves, roughly
½ teaspoon ground cumin	chopped
½ teaspoon sugar	½ yellow (or red) pepper, grilled,
2 tablespoons olive oil	skinned and chopped
1 red onion, peeled and finely chopped	salt, pepper
10–12 black olives (preferably	4 large (or 8 small) lamb chops
Kalamata), pitted and chopped	

1. Place the wine, garlic, cumin and sugar in to a saucepan and bring to the boil. Boil for 5–10 minutes, until the amount of liquid has reduced by half. Then pour into a bowl and cool.
2. Then add the next 6 ingredients and stir well to combine. Season with salt and pepper. Cover and leave for an hour at room temperature.
3. Shortly before serving, preheat the grill to hot and grill the lamb, to your liking. Serve with the compôte. NOTE: Do not freeze.

Chocolate and Mint Cake

The combination of chocolate and mint is not exactly original, but it is still a great favourite and this cake is really rather good, although it is fairly rich.

Cake	Icing
8 oz/250 g caster sugar	3 oz/75 g bitter chocolate
2 tablespoons mint leaves	1 tablespoon mint leaves, finely chopped
4 oz/125 g unsalted butter, softened	4 oz/125 g butter, softened
2 oz/50 g cocoa powder, sieved	5 oz/150 g icing sugar, sifted
2 eggs, beaten	2 oz/50 g ricotta
8 oz/250 g self-raising flour, sifted	
4 fl oz/125 ml boiling water	
a few drops of crème de menthe (optional)	

1. Preheat the oven to Gas Mark 4/180°C/350°F, and butter and flour two 8 in/20 cm sandwich tins. Place the sugar and mint leaves in a food processor, fitted with the metal blade. Process for a few seconds. Change over to the plastic blade.
2. Add the butter and process until well mixed. Add the cocoa, process briefly, then add the eggs, half the flour and half the water. Process for a few seconds, scrape down the sides, then add the remaining flour and water. Blend together for only a short time, until well mixed. Pour into the sandwich tins and bake for 20–25 minutes, until ready. Invert onto wire racks to cool.
4. Meanwhile, make the icing. Melt the chocolate, then set it aside to cool slightly. Chop the mint finely, then beat it into the butter. Add the icing sugar and beat until it is light and fluffy. Finally, mix in the chocolate and ricotta and combine well until smooth.
5. Prick all over the bottom layer of the cake with a fork, then carefully drizzle over a few drops of crème de menthe. Sandwich together with half the icing, then spread the rest on the top. NOTE: This can be frozen, before you have iced it.

Chocolate Bread and Butter Pudding

This is bread and butter pudding with a difference! Firstly, the bread is not bread, but buttery, chocolate-filled pains au chocolat, which we only ever used to enjoy on holiday in France. Nowadays, they are to be found in most supermarkets. These are split and topped with even more chocolate – as bitter as possible (look for a cocoa solids content of at least 55 per cent; preferably 60–70 per cent). The custard is based on milk and cream which has been infused with fresh mint and cardamom pods. Cardamon is a spice which I got to know not in the Middle East or India, where it is widely used in spicy dishes, but in Finland, where it is used in cakes and buns. The famous Finnish pulla, flavoured with cardamom, is a sweet, rich bun, common to Finnish households. There cardamon is bought already ground but, for this pudding, I like to crush the pods roughly in a pestle and mortar. This pudding can be served with cream, but it is so light in texture (not, I fear, in calories!), that it eats very well on its own. (serves 4)

3–4 pains au chocolat (I use 3, but they are fairly large)
1½ oz/40 g bitter chocolate, grated
4 cardamom pods, roughly crushed
½ oz/15 g mint leaves
½ pint/300 ml milk
¼ pint/150 ml double cream
2 eggs
1½ oz/40 g caster sugar

1. Butter an oblong baking dish (the one I use measures 11 in/28 cm by 8 in/20 cm). Cut the pains au chocolat in half, lengthwise and place in the dish, side by side. Sprinkle over the grated chocolate.

2. Place the crushed cardamom, mint, milk and cream in a saucepan and bring slowly to the boil. As soon as you see the bubbles, remove from the heat, stir well and cover. Leave to infuse for 30 minutes.

3. Then strain the milk infusion into a bowl and beat in the eggs and sugar. Pour the custard over the chocolate bread in the dish and leave to soak for 30 minutes. Meanwhile, preheat the oven to Gas Mark 4/180°C/350°F.

4. When the soaking is completed place the baking dish in a bain marie (I use a large roasting tin, half filled with hot water) and bake in the preheated oven for about 30–35 minutes, until it is just set. Remove from the bain marie and allow to cool for about 5–10 minutes, then serve.

NOTE: Do not freeze.

Blackcurrant and Mint Slump

When I first came across the recipe title 'Slump' in American cookery books, I was fascinated. There is no mystery to the wonderful title: a scone-like topping gradually slumps into the fruit filling, as it cooks in the oven. Pure and simple . . . and oh, so delicious! Although it is usually made with blueberries in America, I prefer blackcurrants, which are less sweet. Mint and blackcurrants are, like chocolate and mint, a perfect match. (serves 6)

1½ lb/750 g blackcurrants	<u>Scone topping</u>
4 oz/125 g sugar	6 oz/175 g self-raising flour
3 fl oz/90 ml water	1 teaspoon baking powder
1 oz/25 g cornflour, dissolved in	salt
1½ tablespoons water	2 oz/50 g demerara sugar
3 heaped tablespoons mint,	grated zest and juice of 1 large lemon
freshly chopped	2 oz/50 g unsalted butter, melted
8 oz/250 g Mascarpone cream cheese	3 fl oz/90 ml milk
2 oz/50 g caster sugar	

1. Place the blackcurrants and sugar in a saucepan with the water. Bring to the boil, boil for 2 minutes, then stir in the cornflour paste. Reduce the heat and cook for a further 3 minutes. Remove from the heat and stir in the chopped mint. Pour into a round 8 in/20 cm ovenproof dish.

2. Mix the Mascarpone and caster sugar together, until well blended. Then, using 2 dessert-spoons, carefully drop 6 spoonfuls of the Mascarpone mixture over the blackcurrant and mint mixture, trying to space evenly. Resist the temptation to spread the 6 blobs together!

3. Preheat in the oven to Gas Mark 6/200°C/400°F. For the scone topping, sift the flour, baking powder and salt together. Then add the demerara sugar, lemon zest and juice and the melted butter. Add the milk and stir gently, to combine. (Do not overwork this dough.) What you will end up with is a dropping consistency. Then, using 2 spoons, carefully drop 6 spoonfuls of this dough over the 6 Mascarpone blobs. (Do not panic if it does not exactly cover; it is all going to slump anyway!)

4. Place in the middle shelf of the preheated oven and cook for about 25 minutes, until the filling is bubbling and the scone topping has risen and is golden brown.

5. Cool for about 5–10 minutes, then serve. Since there is a luscious Mascarpone blob under each scone, it is not necessary to offer cream with this pudding. NOTE: Do not freeze.

Ginger Mint Ice-cream

This is an intriguing ice-cream. The colour is a pale green and the flavour a subtle combination of ginger and mint. Ginger mint can be added to a number of dessert recipes, one of my favourite being a chocolate and ginger mousse. But then, it is rather obvious that I am a bit of a chocolate fiend! This ice-cream is enhanced by the addition of some finely chopped stem ginger. Although it is not necessary, it does reinforce the gingery theme. If you omit the ginger and use spearmint instead of ginger mint, then you have a very good plain mint ice-cream. I like to serve this one with thin buttery shortbread (made from 6 oz/175 g each of slightly salted butter and sifted plain flour and 2 oz/50 g each of caster sugar and farola (fine semolina) or with a hot chocolate pudding (see next recipe). (serves 4)

1 oz/25 g ginger mint	4 oz/125 g caster sugar
½ pint/300 ml creamy milk	1 heaped tablespoon stem ginger,
¼ pint/150 ml double cream	finely chopped
3 egg yolks	

1. Place the mint, with the milk and cream, in a large saucepan and bring slowly to the boil. As soon as you see the bubbles, remove from the heat and stir well, pressing down on the mint. Cover with a lid and leave to infuse for 30 minutes. Then strain through a sieve.

2. Mix the egg yolks and sugar in a bowl with a whisk, until they are pale and fluffy. Then pour the milk mixture, with the stem of ginger, into the bowl, whisking all the time. Return this to a heavy-based saucepan and cook, over a low heat, until the custard thickens, stirring constantly. (This takes about 5 minutes.)

3. Pour the custard into a shallow bowl, cover closely with clingfilm and cool. Once it is cold, pour it into an ice-cream maker and churn, or into a shallow freezer box and place in the freezer, removing every hour, to beat well. (You should not need to do this more than 3 times.)

Nick's Hot Chocolate Pudding with Mint Ice-cream

This recipe is one of Nick Nairn's (many) specialities. Nick, Scotland's youngest Michelin-starred chef, cooks at Aberfoyle's Braeval Old Mill. In an idyllic rural setting in the Trossachs, the restaurant kitchen produces superb dishes, using the abundant local game, fish and meat. Try these hot chocolate puddings with some creamy mint ice-cream. Leave them somewhere warm for about 5 minutes, when they come out of the oven. By that time, they will have sunk slightly, just enough to allow a little space to dollop in a good spoonful of your home-made mint ice-cream. (serves 4)

Puddings	Ice-cream
5 oz/150 g bitter chocolate, grated	Make exactly as for ginger mint
(look for at least 55 per cent cocoa	ice-cream, replacing the gingermint
solids; preferably 70 per cent)	by spearmint and omitting the
1 egg yolk plus 5 egg whites	chopped stem ginger.
2 oz/50 g caster sugar	
butter, for smearing	

1. For the puddings, melt the chocolate over a pan of simmering water, then stir in the egg yolk, beating until it thickens slightly. Remove from the heat and cool for a couple of minutes.

2. Meanwhile, preheat the oven to Gas Mark 6/200°C/400°F. Whisk the egg whites until stiff, then gradually fold in the sugar and continue whisking until glossy and thick.

3. Mix a tablespoon of the egg whites into the chocolate, and when they are well blended, gently fold in the remaining egg whites, using a cutting and folding action. Divide the mixture between the prepared ramekins and place on an oven tray. Bake in the preheated oven for 12 minutes.

4. Remove them from the oven and keep somewhere warm. Allow to sink slightly, and serve after about 5 minutes. Offer a bowl of the mint ice-cream with the puddings and suggest that your guests spoon some ice-cream into the middle of the hot puddings. Alternatively, you can invert the puddings on to dessert plates - this leaves room for extra ice-cream! Be warned – there will be calls of 'encore'! NOTE: The puddings cannot be frozen.

chapter 11

oregano

Oregano and marjoram are very closely related. The Latin name for marjoram is *Oreganum majorana*, or *Oreganum onites*; oregano's botanical name is *Oreganum vulgare*, or wild marjoram. Although they have similar characteristics, marjoram is much softer and mellow, whereas oregano has a decidedly pungent, dominating flavour. As a general rule, the two are fairly interchangeable, but whereas marjoram can be used with gay abandon, oregano should be used with a certain amount of caution.

A perennial, oregano grows to a height of about 2½ feet, preferring dry, chalky soils, particularly in scrubland or chalk downs. Although it grows wild in Britain, it is not nearly as pungent as the same plant which grows around the Mediterranean. There, the herb has a peppery taste, which is wonderfully aromatic.

Like so many other herbs, oregano too has a long history of culinary, remedial and medicinal uses. The Ancient Greeks planted oregano plants on graves, as they believed the strong aromas brought pleasure to the dead. Then the Romans used it in marriage ceremonies, intertwined with other herbs to make symbolic crowns, which were placed on the heads of a bride and groom: the herb was believed to bring great and everlasting happiness. In the Middle Ages, oregano, as well as lavender, was used to fill sweet-smelling little purses or bags. This was not only for its strong, aromatic fragrance, but also because it was renowned as an antiseptic.

In Italy and Greece, oregano is generally sold in bundles at markets, for use in all sorts of Mediterranean-style dishes. Having such a dominant taste, it goes particularly well with strong flavours. It is used, both raw and cooked, with tomatoes, beans, aubergines, courgettes, peppers, fish, shellfish and many sorts of meat. It is also good in cheese dishes, meatloaves, rissoles, rice recipes, pastas and pizzas. Although dried oregano is often sprinkled over pizzas, once you try the real thing, it adds a whole new dimension to plain cheese and tomato pizza! Although I have given a recipe for a pizza topped with spicy sausage and pepper (see page 93), you can enliven any pizza topping: try some chopped oregano over Feta cheese and grilled aubergine; or clams, shrimps and garlic; or barbecued chicken and smoked Mozzarella.

Also, try sprinkling some of the freshly chopped leaves on a joint of meat such as lamb or pork, just before roasting. Instead of using basil in a tomato salad, shred over a few leaves of fresh oregano, and drizzle with some fruity olive oil. Many pasta dishes benefit from the addition of oregano. For example, chop some leaves into spaghetti served with a tomato, meat or fish sauce; macaroni served with a cheese sauce made from Parmesan, Cheddar and Mozzarella; or mix with minced lamb and tomatoes and use to stuff cannelloni or tortellini. Although dried oregano is one of the more acceptable dried herbs, there is still a vast difference between the fresh and the dried. In Mexico, when it is dried, it is used as part of a flavouring in commercial chilli powders. As we all know, these are rather fiery things, so this gives us an inkling as to the strength of this pungent, aromatic herb.

Slow-baked Tomatoes

This is such a simple dish, the ideal starter for a summer's day. Be sure the tomatoes you use are bursting with flavour and not the greenhouse types which will be far too watery: the end result will not be oily juices, but runny watery juices. The sugar brings out the flavour of fresh tomatoes — try adding a little to fresh tomato soup. The oregano becomes wonderfully crunchy on top of the tomatoes, and in fact takes on a rather different flavour. You could add a clove or two of garlic or some anchovy fillets if you like, but I think that this dish on its own, served with some freshly-baked, warm crusty bread for mopping up, is perfect. (serves 4 as a starter)

4 large flavoursome tomatoes
1 teaspoon sugar
2 tablespoons extra-virgin olive oil
3 heaped tablespoons oregano, freshly chopped
sea salt

1. Preheat the oven to Gas Mark 1/140°C/275°F. Cut the tomatoes in half and place in an oiled dish, cut-side up. Sprinkle with the sugar, then slowly drizzle over the oil. Top each tomato with some of the chopped oregano and grind over some sea salt.
2. Bake in the preheated oven for 60–75 minutes, until the tomatoes are cooked and the oregano is crispy. Serve warm, with plenty warm bread. NOTE: Do not freeze.

Arbroath Smokie and Parsnip Salad

Both the fish and the parsnips have a rather smoky, nutty flavour which go well with a hazelnut dressing. The oregano adds a lot of punch, as it is wonderfully peppery. By chopping some into the dressing which coats the hot parsnips and by tossing some into the salad just before serving, you have the two textures of oregano: one freshly chopped and the other wilted by the heat. It is not only the colour, but also the flavour which is altered slightly. Be careful not to overcook the parsnips — they should not, by any means, be crunchy (undercooked root vegetables are not very palatable), but if you forget about them, they become too soft and lose their shape when tossed into the dressing. The sun-dried tomatoes to use for this recipe are those already marinated in olive oil, and you can put some of the oil from the jar in the dressing, to reinforce the flavours. As a main course, serve either with freshly baked cheese scones or potato bread, with just a suggestion of butter. (serves 4 as a main course; 6 as a starter)

1 pair of Arbroath Smokies
1½ lb/750 g parsnips, peeled
mixed salad leaves (oakleaf, cos,
   radicchio, lamb's lettuce), prepared
2 tablespoons sun-dried tomatoes,
   chopped
2 tablespoons oregano, freshly
   chopped

Dressing
1 tablespoon oil from the sun-dried
   tomato jar
3 tablespoons hazelnut oil
1 tablespoon lemon juice
salt, pepper
2 tablespoons oregano, freshly
   chopped

1. Warm the smokies slightly (either for 10–15 minutes at Gas Mark 2/150°C/300°F or for 2 minutes in a microwave on high), then peel off the skin. Remove the flesh and flake into chunks.

2. Meanwhile make the dressing by shaking all the dressing ingredients in a screw-top jar.

3. Cut the parsnips into matchsticks, drop into boiling water, and cook for 2-4 minutes depending on the thickness of the matchsticks. Drain when just tender and toss into the dressing while still warm.

4. Place the salad leaves into a large bowl, top with the sun-dried tomatoes, then the oregano.

5. Just before serving, toss the dressed parsnips, with all the dressing, into the salad bowl, add the chunks of fish and gently toss everything together. Serve at once.

NOTE: Do not freeze.

Spicy Sausage and Pepper Pizza

Pizza is a great favourite with my ever-hungry children, and I like to introduce them to new flavours instead of the usual tomato, cheese and mushrooms. Making the base is easy, but it does require a little bit of elbow grease: kneading, which gives enormous satisfaction! You can resort to a food processor and dough hooks, which will knead the dough for you. I love using fresh yeast for its smell and texture, but appreciate easy-blend dried yeast is a life-saver. It should always be mixed directly with the dry flour, before the water is introduced. There are various types of spicy sausage around. I like to use either kabanos (a Polish, lightly smoked sausage) or chorizo (a Spanish, spicy smoked sausage); whatever you use, make sure it is a cured sausage which requires no further cooking. The grilled peppers add a wonderful colour and taste to the final result. You can add some pitted black olives at the end if you like. (serves 4–6)

Base	Topping
1 lb/500 g strong white flour	2 peppers (red or orange), deseeded and quartered
1 level teaspoon easy-blend dried yeast	
1 teaspoon salt	2 tablespoons passata (thick, sieved tomatoes)
2 tablespoons olive oil, plus oil for greasing	8 oz/250 g spicy sausage, cut into chunks
½ pint/300 ml tepid water	4 oz/125 g grated Mozzarella cheese
	2 tablespoons oregano
	2 tablespoons extra-virgin olive oil

1. For the base, place the flour, yeast and salt in a bowl. Make a well in the middle, pour in the oil, then sufficient water to combine to a soft dough. Remove the dough to a floured board and knead for about 10 minutes, until it feels smooth. Put it in an oiled bowl, cover and place somewhere warm (e.g., an airing cupboard) for 1–1½ hours, or until it has doubled in size.

3. Meanwhile grill the peppers until charred, then wrap tightly in foil and leave for 20 minutes. Remove the foil and peel off the skins. Cut the peppers into slivers.

4. Tip the risen dough on to the board again, and punch it down with your fists. Then, using both hands, push the dough into the required shape on an oiled baking tray (mine is 9 in/ 23 cm by 13 in/33 cm).

5. Spread the passata on to the dough, then top with the sausage, peppers and cheese. Tear (or chop) the oregano and sprinkle over the top. Drizzle over 2 tablespoons of olive oil and set aside for 30 minutes, somewhere warm, until puffy around the edges. Preheat the oven to Gas Mark 7/220°C/425°F. Bake in the preheated oven for about 20 minutes until golden brown and well-risen. Serve at once.

NOTE: Do not freeze.

Prawns with Oregano

For this dish you will need uncooked jumbo or tiger prawns. I buy frozen ones from my fishmonger when fresh are unavailable. Defrost them slowly in the fridge, rather than at room temperature. The cooking time is for prawns which weigh (unshelled) about 2 oz/50 g each. I suggest about 3 for each person as a starter. To shell prawns, simply peel off the thin shell; the tiny legs will come away too. With a sharp knife, slit half way down the front, open out slightly and locate the intestinal tract, which is a long black thread. Either carefully and slowly pull it out with your finger and thumb, or scrape it out with the tip of a knife. Then wash them under running water and pat them dry with kitchen paper. The prawns should be cooked for only a couple of minutes. Serve hot with some warm pitta bread. (serves 3 as a starter)

1–1¼ lb/500–625 g large raw prawns, shelled and cleaned	juice of 1 lemon
1oz/25 g butter	4 tablespoons oregano, freshly chopped
1 tablespoon olive oil	freshly ground black pepper

1. Make sure the prawns are well cleaned and dry. Then heat the butter and oil in a large frying pan until very hot. Add the prawns and fry for about 1 minute on each side (no more than 3 minutes altogether). They are ready when their colour changes from clear to off-white/pink.

2. Mix the lemon juice and oregano in a bowl. Toss in the prawns and the pan juices, grind over plenty of black pepper and serve at once. NOTE: Do not freeze.

Couscous and Oregano-stuffed Fish

Red snapper, red tilapia, strawberry grouper or sea bass are all good for this recipe. If the fish is much heavier than the weight below, simply increase the cooking times accordingly. Couscous is good made into a salad or as a stuffing for fish or vegetables. This enhances the flavour even more. All I would serve with the fish is a couscous salad, spiked with plenty of garlic, parsley and lemon, and some fresh crusty bread. This recipe is sufficient for 2 people, or is a generous portion for one good appetite. (serves 1–2)

1 medium whole fish (about 10 oz/300 g) gutted and scaled	1 shallot, peeled and finely chopped
olive oil	1 garlic clove, peeled and chopped
6 large oregano leaves	1 heaped tablespoon oregano, freshly chopped
1 oz/25 g couscous	salt, pepper
2 tablespoons lemon juice	1 tablespoon extra-virgin olive oil

1. Using a very sharp knife or scissors, cut 3 slashes in each side of the fish. Tuck in a large oregano leaf into each, then rub olive oil over the whole fish and place in a baking dish.

2. For the stuffing, place the couscous in a bowl with the lemon juice, shallot, garlic and oregano. Stir well, season with salt and pepper, then cover and leave to soak for 20 minutes. Preheat the oven to Gas mark 5/190°C/375°F.

3. Carefully stuff the fish with the couscous, pour over the olive oil and bake, uncovered, in the preheated oven for about 25 minutes, or until the fish is cooked (check after 20 minutes with the tip of a knife). Baste once during cooking.

4. It can be served immediately but I prefer to allow it to rest for about 10 minutes. NOTE: Do not freeze.

Chilli, Onion and Oregano Polenta

Polenta, which is coarsely ground maize meal, has left its natural home in the northern plains of Italy to become fashionable in Britain. I love its bright yellow colour and porridge-like consistency. My method of cooking polenta would fill the average Italian with horror. The 'correct' way is to bring the water to the boil, then pour in the polenta in a very slow stream, whisking or stirring constantly. It is traditionally cooked for anything up to 45 minutes, but by using the new 'pre-cooked' variety, it cooks in 5–10 minutes. Serve it to accompany a dressed salad, or with a fresh tomato sauce as a starter or light lunch; alternatively cut it neatly into diamond shapes and serve them hot, as an unusual canapé. (serves 6–8)

1 tablespoon olive oil	1 teaspoon salt
1 large onion, peeled and finely chopped	3 heaped tablespoons oregano, freshly chopped
1 large or 2 small fresh red chillis, deseeded, finely chopped	2 oz/50 g butter, melted
8 oz/250 g (pre-cooked/quick-cooking) polenta	2 ½ oz/65 g freshly grated Parmesan cheese
1½ pints/1 litre cold water	salt, pepper
	extra-virgin olive oil (optional)

1. Heat the oil in a frying pan. Gently fry the onion for about 10 minutes, until softened and golden brown. Add the chilli and cook for a further 2 minutes.

2. Meanwhile, place the polenta and water in a large saucepan with the salt. Bring very slowly to the boil, stirring (I prefer whisking) all the time. Once it has started bubbling, reduce the heat and, whisking occasionally, simmer for 5 minutes (or according to the packet instructions). By this time, it should be thick, like porridge.

3. Tip in the entire contents of the onion and chilli pan, then add the oregano, melted butter and cheese. Stir well to combine and season to taste. Remove from the heat. Either serve now or pour the contents into a buttered 2 lb/1 kg loaf tin, smooth out the top and chill for several hours.

4. Once it is completely cold, turn it out and carefully cut into thin slices. Brush these with olive oil and place under a preheated grill for 3–4 minutes each side, until golden and toasted. Serve at once. NOTE: Do not freeze.

Oregano Dumplings

These can be made with a variety of herbs: parsley, chives, marjoram or savory are all good. Do not worry about the prospect of lead-heavy dumplings – these ones should be fairly light, as long as they are cooked all the way through, and given a flash under the grill to make the top crunchy and golden brown. Add the water little by little to the mixture, working it very gently with your hand until it becomes a softish dough, which leaves the sides of the bowl clean. Once you get the hang of making herb dumplings, you can use them to top any other hearty stews, casseroles or hotpots. (makes 5–6)

4 oz/125 g self-raising flour	2 tablespoons oregano, finely chopped
2 oz/50 g shredded suet	about 5 tablespoons water
salt, pepper	

1. Sift the flour into a bowl and add the suet, salt, pepper and oregano. Mix well.
2. Gradually add some cold water, just sufficient to make a soft dough, similar to a scone dough.
3. Divide the dough into 5 or 6, then roll into balls, using floured hands.
4. If they are to top a stew or casserole proceed as in steps 4 to 6 of the recipe below; adding the dumplings for the last 30 minutes of cooking at a fairly high temperature. The perfect dumplings should be cooked all the way through and golden brown on top.

NOTE: Do not freeze.

Oxtail with Anchovies and Oregano

Oxtail stew is comfort food. That is why I suggest serving it with crusty, herby dumplings, although it would also be delicious with creamy mashed potatoes or butter-bean purée. After eating this dish all will be well with the world, I assure you! Before you cook the oxtail, be sure it is well trimmed of fat, otherwise there will be a greasy layer on top of the casserole. The addition of anchovies with the oxtail might seem bizarre but, in fact, their salty, savoury taste means an added depth of flavour, without any fishy overtones. The oregano adds a good spicy tone to the dish, which is also enhanced by some tangy orange zest. The oxtail dish is good on its own (in which case, do not raise the oven temperature, but give it a full 2 hours' cooking at the lower setting), but I would recommend the dumplings, for a trip down memory lane. (serves 4)

3 lb/1.25 g oxtail, cut unto 2 in/5 cm pieces, trimmed of as much fat as possible	4 large (or 6 medium) anchovy fillets, chopped
1 tablespoon olive oil	½ pint/300 ml beef stock
1 large onion, peeled and chopped	salt, pepper
2 garlic cloves, peeled and chopped	2 tablespoons oregano, chopped
¼ pint/150 ml red wine	zest of 1 small orange

1. Preheat the oven to Gas Mark 3/160°C/375°F. Heat a large, heavy ovenproof casserole until very hot indeed. Add the oxtail and brown all over without extra fat, then remove with a slotted spoon.
2. Add the oil to the casserole, then gently fry the onion and garlic for 2–3 minutes, until softened. Pour in the wine, bring to the boil, then add the anchovies and boil for 2 minutes. Add the stock, orange zest and oregano, return the oxtail, season with a little salt and pepper, cover the casserole and lower the heat.
3. Place the casserole in a preheated oven for 1½ hours, stirring every 30 minutes.
4. Remove and check the seasoning, adding more salt if necessary, then increase the oven temperature to Gas Mark 6/200°C/400°F.
5. Pop the herb dumplings on top of the casserole (on the sauce, not the actual meat). Place in the oven, uncovered, for 25–30 minutes, until the dumplings are cooked.
6. Flash the casserole under a very hot grill for about 2 minutes, to make the dumplings golden and crunchy on top, then serve at once, straight from the casserole.

NOTE: The oxtail (without the dumplings) can be frozen after checking the seasoning in step 4.

chapter 12

parsley

Our most common culinary herb, parsley (*Petroselinum crispum*), needs little introduction. A hardy biennial, it adapts well to almost every climate and soil-type, but it does fare best in a well-drained, fairly rich soil. Although there are many varieties, the two we are familiar with are curly-leaved and French (or flat-leaved) parsley. The former is widely grown, primarily as a garnish, but also chopped into sauces or stews. If you 'blind-taste' the two, you will detect at once why the flat-leaf parsley is invariably the choice of chefs. Although the two taste very similar, the flat-leaf has a superior flavour, without the rather harsh aftertaste and coarse texture of the curly-leaved. In the following recipes, flat parsley should be used in preference to curly parsley if possible. Otherwise, you should chop curly parsley more finely than flat-leaf.

I have steered away from the use of parsley merely as a garnish. I garnish when the colour (pale, insipid) or texture (soft) of the food requires strengthening; curly parsley might pass as acceptable garnish to a dish which makes no use of the herb in the actual cooking process. Primarily, however, a garnish should always be relevant to the food which it is decorating. But once you have used parsley for its taste – not simply its decorative qualities – then you will see how versatile a herb it is.

Rich in vitamins A and C, and iron, parsley has long been used in the kitchen and also as a medicine. Parsley tea was often prescribed for kidney problems, rheumatism or jaundice. The Ancient Greeks used to make wreaths of parsley entwined with hyacinths for special occassions, such as Menelaus' marriage feast, as recorded by Homer.

Its uses in the kitchen are endless. One excellent use of curly-leafed parsley is to wash and dry it, then deep-fry it in oil until crunchy; this makes the most superb accompaniment to fried fish. Otherwise, as already stated, use flat-leaf, which has a better flavour. It goes with all types of fish; do not forget those old favourites, tartare sauce and hot parsley sauce.

Parsley is also essential in herb or garlic butters and in 'persillade', which is a mixture of parsley and shallot, added to many French dishes towards the end of cooking. In Italy, it becomes with the addition of grated lemon zest 'gremolata', and is sprinkled over that classic dish, Ossobuco; I also use it to top hearty oxtail stews or roast leg of lamb. Parsley salads, made only with chopped leaves dressed in oil and lemon are unusual and delicious, as is parsley pesto, served with freshly cooked pasta, as a change from basil pesto. Use it generously in vegetable soups, omelettes, mayonnaises, risottos or patés. Any dish which contains garlic cries out for parsley, because it softens the rather harsh flavour of the garlic. Chewing on leaves of parsley is possibly the best antidote to that dreadful raw garlic aftertaste – preferable to packets of peppermints, which can ruin your teeth anyway. For so many reasons, therefore, parsley is the one herb your garden cannot do without.

Parsley Soup

This soup is a perfect example of how to make full use of our most popular herb, stalks and all. When cutting off the leaves to use in recipes, never throw away the stalks: they are invaluable in stocks, marinades and soups. Usually, they are removed before serving, but in this soup they are puréed up with the other ingredients, as a vegetable. The result is a tasty, thick green soup. The secret is only in liquidising everything together, so the vegetables and herbs are well blended. (serves 4–6)

2 oz/50 g butter	1 large leek, washed and sliced
1 onion, peeled and chopped	5 oz/150 g parsley stalks and leaves
2 sticks celery, chopped	1½ pints/900 ml light chicken stock
1 lb/500 g potatoes, peeled and chopped	½ teaspoon salt
	pepper

1. Heat the butter in a large saucepan, then gently fry the onion, celery, potatoes and leek for about 10 minutes. Add the parsley, stock, salt and pepper, bring to the boil, cover and simmer for about 30 minutes.

2. Whizz everything together in a liquidiser (a food processor will do, but you might need to sieve it afterwards), then taste for seasoning.

4. Serve piping hot, perhaps with a swirl of cream and freshly chopped parsley.

NOTE: The soup freezes well.

Mozzarella and Garlic Bread

These toasts are delicious, served piping hot either as a snack lunch or supper or, cut into quarters, as canapés to go with drinks, the only problem being that they are so moreish; there is a grave danger of appetites being greatly diminished if they are the prelude to a hearty dinner. For the bread, try to find a close-textured country-style loaf. The Italian country bread used for bruschetta or crostini is ideal. Ciabatta, which is widely available in our supermarkets, works fairly well, although it is more open-textured. It is important to use extra-virgin olive oil for this – the fruitier the better – as the flavour comes through strongly. The garlic is, for once, not overpowering, as all you do is rub a cut clove over the toast before topping with the cheese and parsley. Although it is not essential, I also like to rub a cut tomato into the toast to make it even more moist. (makes 6 slices)

6 slices country bread	2 heaped tablespoons parsley, freshly chopped
1 garlic clove, peeled and cut in half	3 oz/75 g grated Mozzarella cheese
1 small ripe tomato, cut in half	
3–4 tablespoons extra-virgin olive oil	

1. Place the bread under a hot grill until toasted on one side. Turn the slices over and very lightly toast them, until they just begin to harden, but before they take on too much colour.

2. Remove the grill-pan. Rub the cut garlic on to the lightly toasted side of each slice. Then, with the cut side of the tomato, repeat the procedure. Sprinkle the oil over each slice. Mix together the cheese and parsley and divide between the 6 slices, spreading over the lightly toasted side.

3. Grill again for 2–3 minutes, until bubbling hot. Serve at once.

NOTE: Do not freeze.

Parsley Pasty

Cornish pasties are probably the most perfect of all picnic foods. My recipe makes one rather large pasty, which easily feeds 2 people. You can make 2 smaller ones if you prefer, but it is difficult to achieve such a moist filling if they are smaller. The parsley pasty is based on a recipe from The Lizard Pasty Shop, the most southerly Cornish pasty shop. The traditional filling is made only with skirt beef, onion, swede and potato, which should all be very well seasoned. The pastry, made from strong white bread flour is light, crisp and flaky. I have added chopped parsley to the pastry dough and some whole parsley leaves to the filling; I think the flavour is greatly enhanced, but I realise my opinion might not go down too well in Cornwall. The 'crimping' technique used to seal the pasty makes the final product look authentic. It is not difficult: simply fold the pastry edge over in a rope pattern, tucking in the end when you reach the other side. It is important not to prick a hole in the top before baking, for the filling is almost 'pressure-cooked' with the juices all sealed inside, to provide the most succulent pasty. (makes 1 large pasty)

Pastry
8 oz/250 g strong white flour, sifted
½ teaspoon salt
1 tablespoon parsley, freshly chopped
4 oz/125 g butter and white fat, cubed
1½–2 tablespoons cold water

Filling (prepared or peeled weights)
1 oz/25 g onion, finely chopped
2 oz/50 g swede, finely chopped
salt, pepper
3–4 oz/75–125 g skirt beef, cut into small pieces
5–6 sprigs flat parsley
4–5 oz/125–150 g potatoes, finely chopped
beaten egg or milk, to glaze

1. To make the pastry place the flour, salt and parsley in the food processor and process briefly. Then add the fats and process until they resemble breadcrumbs, before adding sufficient water to combine into a ball. Otherwise sift the flour and salt together in a bowl, add the parsley and rub in the fats until the mixture resembles breadcrumbs. Then add just enough water to combine. Cover and refrigerate for about 30 minutes.

2. Preheat to Gas Mark 7/220°C/425°F. Roll out the pastry to about 9 in/23 cm round. Trim around the edges with a plate, to form a neat circle. Place the onion and turnip on the semi-circle of the pastry which will form the bottom of the pasty, then season well. Place the meat on top, season again, then top with whole parsley leaves. Top with the potatoes and season again. Press the filling down well as you go.

3. Moisten one half of the circle edge with water, then fold over the other half to seal. 'Crimp' the edges. Do not prick a 'steam' hole.

4. Transfer to a lightly greased baking tray and brush with egg or milk to glaze. Bake in a preheated oven for 10 minutes, then turn the oven down to Gas Mark 4/180°C/350°F for a further 45 minutes. Serve warm (never hot) or cold.

NOTE: Do not freeze.

Sun-dried Tomato Risotto

It is essential to use arborio (risotto) rice to make really good risottos, for the grains hold their shape, retain their firm bite, yet take on a wonderfully creamy texture. The other essential about cooking risotto is to make sure your stock is very hot or boiling, as you gradually add it by the ladleful. You can - and indeed should - let risotto stand for about 10 minutes, once you have stirred in the Parmesan, but it is best not done longer than half an hour in advance. The sun-dried tomatoes I like to use are those preserved in olive oil, so you can incorporate the oil into the recipe. You can marinate the tomatoes in oil yourself; soak sun-dried tomatoes in warm water for an hour or so, then pat them as dry as possible. Layer them in a wide-necked jar, with sprigs of rosemary or thyme and best-quality olive oil. If possible, leave for about a week before using. Serve it with tossed salad and a glass of Chianti. (serves 4)

4 tablespoons olive oil, from the jar of tomatoes
2 garlic cloves, peeled and chopped
1 small onion, peeled and chopped
8 oz/250 g arborio rice
4 tablespoons sun-dried tomatoes, cut into small pieces
4 oz/125 g small button mushrooms
1¼ pints/750 ml hot chicken stock
4 heaped tablespoons parsley, freshly chopped
2 oz/50 g freshly grated Parmesan
salt, pepper
Parmesan shavings, to serve

1. Heat the oil in a saucepan and gently fry the garlic and onion for a couple of minutes.
2. Add the rice, stir well to coat with the oil, then add the tomatoes and mushrooms. Cook for a minute or two, until everything is well coated.
3. One ladle at a time, gradually add the hot stock, stirring well with each addition. After about 15 minutes, add the parsley and continue to simmer until the grains are just cooked. (You may not need all the stock.)
4. Add the Parmesan, season to taste with salt and pepper, then cover and allow to stand, off the heat, for about 10 minutes. Sprinkle the Parmesan shavings over the top and serve.

NOTE: Do not freeze.

Chickpea Salad

This is based on a Lebanese salad, 'balila', which is strongly flavoured with onion and parsley and dressed only with lemon juice. I have made the after-taste less pungent by adding shallot instead of onion, the extra sweetness of tomato and just a hint of oil, to lessen the sharpness of the lemon juice. This dish can be served as part of a selection of hors d'oeuvres ('mazet' in Lebanon), with marinated vegetables or salads redolent of fresh mint or coriander. Or serve it a vegetarian dish on its own, with plenty of warm fresh bread. (serves 3–4)

1 x 14 oz/425 g tin cooked chickpeas
4 heaped tablespoons parsley
2 shallots, peeled and finely chopped
2 garlic cloves, peeled and crushed
juice of 1 large lemon
1 large tomato, peeled and diced
1 tablespoon extra-virgin olive oil
salt, pepper

1. Drain the chickpeas well and place in a bowl. Roughly chop the parsley (not too finely), then add to the bowl.
2. Mix in all the other ingredients, seasoning with salt and pepper according to taste. Serve at room temperature, not straight from the fridge. NOTE: Do not freeze.

Spaghetti Marinara

There are many variations of that most wonderfully tasty, yet simple dish, Spaghetti Marinara. You can vary the type of seafood you use according to season or availability. Add prawns, langoustines or chunks of tuna, if you like. To make things easy, I have stipulated the use of already cooked seafood, so if you feel particularly lazy, you can use a jar or tin of clams, cockles or mussels; but with the proviso that they must all be rinsed well, so there is no hint of vinegar or brine, then patted dry gently with kitchen paper. If, however, there is a plethora of inviting-looking fresh mussels or clams in the fishmongers, then scrub them very well, and steam them for 2–3 minutes, until the shells open. (Discard any which resolutely remain shut.) Wait until they are cool enough to handle, then remove from their shells and proceed as stated in the recipe. There is a hint of chilli and garlic in the sauce, to enhance the seafood and the parsley porvides not only good colour and taste, but softens the potential pungency of both garlic and chilli. Do not offer Parmesan with this dish. (serves 4)

12–14 oz/375–425 g spaghetti
4 tablespoons olive oil
3 garlic cloves, peeled and chopped
½ small fresh green chilli, deseeded
3 anchovy fillets, mashed with a fork
4 tablespoons dry white wine
12 oz/375 g mixed clams, mussels, cockles (cooked and well-drained, if necessary)
5 tablespoons parsley, freshly chopped
salt, pepper

1. Cook the spaghetti according to packet instructions. When cooked, drain well and toss in 1 tablespoon olive oil.
2. Heat the remaining 3 tablespoons of oil in a large pan, then gently fry the garlic and chilli for 1 minute. Add the anchovies and wine, increase the heat and bubble away for 2–3 minutes.
3. Reduce the heat, then add the clams, cockles and mussels. Stir well and cook gently for another 4–5 minutes, until the seafood is heated through. Add the parsley, then remove from the heat. Season salt and pepper to taste, then toss the spaghetti into the frying pan, mix well and serve at once. NOTE: Do not freeze.

Potato and Parsnip Hash

This is a variation on a theme. It is not quite corned beef hash but it is vaguely reminiscent of Scottish stovies, which are a mixture of onion and potatoes fried in beef dripping, often topped with corned beef or leftover roast meat chopped in towards the end. Stovies, however, are cooked 'stoved' in a covered pan, with the minimal amount of stirring; I find shaking the pan boldly is the best way to avoid it all sticking to the bottom. This potato and parsnip hash is cooked in a large frying pan and is best served straight from the pan, strewn with some freshly torn parsley leaves. Top it with fried eggs, and it definitely fits into the category of wholesome and comforting food. (serves 4)

8 oz/250 g parsnips
1 lb/500 g potatoes
2 tablespoons olive oil
1 oz/25 g butter
1 large onion, peeled and sliced
salt, pepper
4 oz/125 g corned beef, roughly chopped
3 heaped tablespoons parsley, freshly chopped
a few sprigs of fresh parsley, to serve

1. Peel the parsnips and potatoes. Leave them whole and cook in salted water for about 15 minutes until just tender.

2. Cool slightly, then cut into thick slices, discarding any woody cores from the parsnips.

3. Heat the oil and butter in a large frying pan. Fry the onion for about 5 minutes, then add the parsnips and potatoes. Fry over a fairly high heat, stirring occasionally, for about 10 minutes. Season well with salt and pepper.

4. Add the corned beef and fry for another 5 minutes, then stir in the parsley and continue to cook for a further 5 minutes.

5. Season again to taste, then serve, topped with freshly chopped or torn parsley leaves.

NOTE: Do not freeze.

Mexican-style Beef

This is wonderfully messy and delicious; definitely food for sharing. There are several bowls of side-dishes, such as sour cream, avocado, lettuce and tomato, to be handed round, for everyone to fill their own tortillas. First of all, it is important to have the right type of tortilla. For this recipe, you need wheat-flour tortillas (which come from Northern Mexico), which are soft; not the more common corn (maize) tortillas, which are usually used for tacos. Wheat tortillas can be bought either from Mexican food specialists or from large supermarkets. The best way to warm them up is on a hot griddle or non-stick frying pan, but, if you wrap them in foil, you can warm them in a low oven. The type of beef I use for this recipe is one of the cheapest but most flavoursome cuts - skirt beef. It should be cut into the thinnest slices you can, with a very sharp knife. A minimum of 2 hours is required to marinate the meat in lime, cumin, soy and Worcestershire sauces, and of course parsley. I use the parsley stalks for the marinade. Then the freshly chopped leaves are added to the beef as it cooks. Have all the accompaniments ready (and your guests seated, Margueritas in hand) before you fry the beef, as it takes literally 2 minutes. (serves 4–5)

1¼ lb/625 g skirt beef, trimmed of outer fat	<u>To fry</u> 2 tablespoons sunflower oil 2 tablespoons parsley, freshly chopped
<u>Marinade</u> juice of 1 lime 1 tablespoon Worcestershire sauce ½ tablespoon light soy sauce ½ teaspoon ground cumin ¼ teaspoon salt 8–10 parsley stalks, broken up pepper	<u>To serve</u> 8–10 wheat flour tortillas, warmed shredded lettuce 1 small tub soured cream 1 large beef tomato, sliced 1 large ripe avocado, cut into slivers and tossed in lemon juice 8–10 wedges of lime

1. Slice the beef as thinly as possible, across the grain, into bite-size pieces. Place in a bowl. Mix the marinade ingredients and pour over the beef, stirring well to combine. Cover and leave for at least 2 hours.

2. Meanwhile, prepare a bowl of shredded lettuce, and one of sour cream. Slice the tomato and prepare the avocado.

3. Remove and discard the parsley stalks from the marinade. Heat the oil in a large frying pan until very hot, then add the meat, the remaining marinade and chopped parsley. Stir-fry for 2–3 minutes, until the meat is just cooked. Place in a warm bowl on the table.

4. To serve, allow each person to assemble their own tortilla: place some meat, then lettuce, sour cream, avocado and tomato on each warm tortilla. Squeeze over a little lime juice. Fold up the lower part of the tortilla, then the sides, to make a parcel. Eat at once.

NOTE: Do not freeze.

chapter 13

rocket

One of the earliest salad leaves of spring, rocket (*Eruca vesicaria*) grows wild in waste places and as a weed on cultivated land. An annual that can be grown easily from seed, it prefers a rich soil and a sunny position. A native of southern Europe, it can now also be found in North America, wild or cultivated. The wild variety does not grow as tall as garden varieties but has the stronger flavour. Rocket is also known as rucola, ruchetta, roquette and aragula.

Commonly used in France and Egypt as an interesting addition to any mixture of salad leaves, the flavour of rocket is piquant, peppery and rather nutty. Rocket's unique taste has also made it a great favourite in Italian salads. In southern Italy, especially in the countryside, it has been used both in salads and in cooked recipes for many years. Only within the last twenty or so years though, has it been discovered in the north of Italy and in the cities. For example, the classic Venetian 'carpaccio' is a dish of very thinly sliced beef served raw with shavings of Parmesan and some rocket leaves, dressed simply with either olive or truffle oil and balsamic vinegar or lemon juice. There is also an equivalent fish carpaccio of thinly sliced smoked salmon served with chopped rocket, dressed in oil and lemon juice. The piquancy of the rocket is ideal with an oily fish such as salmon.

Rocket has now become very fashionable, which means, sadly, it is expensive to buy. In Britain it is not, however, new: the Romans introduced both the leaves and seeds of rocket as flavourings and in Elizabethan England it was used in salads and as a tonic. Rich in vitamin C, it is, in theory, a healthy thing to eat; but since it has a natural affinity with both butter and olive oil, many rocket dishes end up being rather less healthy. However, if served with a light dressing, perhaps a mixture of olive or nut oil with sunflower oil and either lemon juice or wine vinegar, then it becomes a simple, healthy and exciting salad. Indeed, its pungent, almost spicy flavour livens up any mixed leaf salad.

Rocket flowers taste very similar to the leaves and range in colour from white to yellowish, with dark purple veins. They are, therefore, ideal as decoration on a salad of rocket leaves, or you can use them with pasta salads, grilled goat's cheese or cold roast chicken or beef.

Another way of dealing with rocket is to treat it as you might young spinach: cook it for 1–2 minutes in butter or oil and serve as a vegetable. Or you can toss some raw leaves with a spoonful of your best olive oil into freshly cooked pasta: the heat of the pasta is sufficient to 'cook', or rather wilt, the rocket. Another pasta idea comes from Liguria, northern Italy, where 'pansotti' are made. These are ravioli filled with a mixture of herbs, Ricotta, Parmesan and garlic. The herbs, usually a combination of rocket, marjoram and borage, are blanched, chopped and well-seasoned before being mixed with the cheeses. In Puglia, southern Italy, a dish of rocket, potatoes and pasta (usually macaroni) is served with a tomato sauce laced with chilli peppers. It is called 'bandiera' (flag) for it incorporates the green, white and red of the Italian flag.

Rocket and Butternut Squash Soup

Here is an example of rocket used as a vegetable. Rocket goes remarkably well with squash in this thick orange and green speckled soup. If you cannot find squash, substitute the same weight of pumpkin. To prepare butternut squash, stand it right way up and cut in half horizontally. Then peel off the thick skin, with a sharp knife. The seeds are in the fatter lower section; using a serrated spoon, gouge them out and discard them. Then chop the bright orange flesh and proceed. The rocket wilts rather than cooks, but adds a vivid green colour and fresh flavour to the soup just before serving. You can use older, tougher leaves for this recipe. (serves 6)

1 oz/25g butter
1 onion, peeled and chopped
2 garlic cloves, peeled and chopped
1 butternut squash (about 2 lb/1 kg weight before peeling)
5 oz/150 g rocket stalks and leaves (washed if necessary)
1½ pints/900 ml light chicken stock
salt, pepper

1. Melt the butter in a large saucepan. Gently fry the onion and garlic for a couple of minutes.
2. Peel the squash and cut into cubes. Add these to the pan and stir to coat with the butter. Cook for 3 minutes.
3. Add about three-quarters of the rocket, then pour in the stock. Bring to the boil, and then reduce to a simmer. Cook gently for about 25 minutes, until the squash is tender.
4. Either liquidise or blend in a blender (or use a hand-held blender) until smooth and thick.
5. Return to the heat. Roughly chop or tear the remaining rocket leaves and add to the soup. Cook for 1 minute, stirring all the time, then season to taste. Serve at once, piping hot.

NOTE: Although the taste is still good, the colour is not so bright after freezing.

Rocket and Parmesan Salad

This salad can be served as a first course, on its own, or to accompany a main course such as pan-fried steak, grilled salmon fillets or roast chicken. Wash the rocket leaves only if necessary. If they are fresh from the garden, they should not require washing. Make sure they are dry before adding the dressing, otherwise the oil will not adhere to the delicate leaves. In the recipe, the weight of Parmesan is that after shaving off the curls. To make the curls, use a swivel potato peeler and run it down a block of Parmesan (use a wedge of mature Parmigiano Reggiano). Once you have mastered this technique, use the Parmesan curls to top all sorts or pasta dishes, or indeed any dish which incorporates Parmesan. (serves 3–4)

3–4 oz/75–125 g young, rocket leaves
1½–2 oz/40–50 g Parmesan shavings
1 tablespoon extra-virgin olive oil
3 tablespoons hazelnut oil
1 tablespoon balsamic vinegar
salt, pepper

1. Roughly tear the rocket leaves and lay them in a salad bowl. Top with three-quarters of the Parmesan shavings.
2. Mix together the oils, vinegar and seasoning to taste, then pour this over the salad. Toss carefully, taking care not to break up the cheese. Top with the remaining Parmesan shavings and serve at once.

NOTE: Do not freeze.

Rocket and Prawn Salad

The flavouring in this salad comes from wasabi, which is sometimes called Japanese horseradish. Although the fresh wasabi root is unlikely to be found outside Japan, you can easily find wasabi powder (which is mixed with water, rather like dried mustard) or wasabi paste. The flavour of wasabi is, unsurprisingly, similar to horseradish, but it is stronger. If you have a bad cold, wasabi is perfect to unblock those sinuses! If you have difficulty finding wasabi, then substitute horseradish relish, but you will need double the amount. Try to get the most succulent-looking prawns you can find; tiger prawns or jumbo prawns. If you have to shell them, simply peel away the shells and check to see if the intestinal tract remains. This is a black thread running down the inside of the prawn. Simply pull it away or tease it out with a tip of a knife. Then wash them, if necessary, toss in lemon juice and serve atop the punchy salad of rocket and lettuce leaves. This makes the most wonderful summer starter, served with freshly baked soda bread. (serves 3–4)

Salad
12–16 large, cooked prawns, unshelled
    and clean
the juice of ½ lemon
salt, pepper
3 oz/75 g rocket leaves
1 crisp lettuce, washed

Dressing
2 tablespoons sunflower oil
2 tablespoons olive oil
juice of ½ lemon
½ teaspoon wasabi paste (or 1 teaspoon horseradish relish)
salt, pepper

1. Place the prepared prawns in a bowl, then turn them in the lemon juice and salt and pepper.
2. Place the rocket and lettuce in a large salad bowl. Shake together all the dressing ingredients in a screw-top jar, then toss over the salad.
3. Top with the prawns and serve at once.

NOTE: Do not freeze.

Fillet of Beef with Rocket Sauce

Since few of us nowadays eat as much red meat as we used to, it is wonderful occasionally to have a treat of some well-hung, nicely marbled beef. It is at its simplest but best when quickly fried and served with a simple tasty sauce. The rocket sauce for this dish is a kind of pesto, but without the addition of garlic which allows the flavour of the rocket to come boldly through. The sauce can also be served on top of baked potatoes, hot pasta or vegetables such as courgettes or green beans. The cooking times for the beef are vague, since we all like our beef done differently. You can check how it is doing by cutting into the steak with a sharp knife. I would serve this dish with some steamed green vegetables and either sauté or boiled new potatoes. A hearty Rioja would also slip down a treat. (serves 4)

3 oz/75 g rocket
3 oz/75 g pine kernels, toasted
2 oz/50 g Parmesan cheese
approximately 6 tablespoons extra-virgin olive oil
salt, pepper
4 x 5-6 oz/150–175 g fillet steaks
1 tablespoon groundnut oil

1. Place the rocket, pine kernels and Parmesan in a food processor and process briefly until well chopped. Slowly add sufficient olive oil to make a thickish paste. Season to taste.

2. Season the steaks well with salt and pepper just before cooking. Heat the groundnut oil in a large frying pan to very hot indeed. Sear the steaks on either side for 2 minutes (the fat will splatter everywhere, but do not be tempted to turn down the heat yet). After the 4 minutes, turn down the heat to medium and continue to cook the steaks for another 3 minutes for rare, about 5 for medium and about 8 for well-done. (Although this, of course, depends on the thickness of the steaks.)

3. To serve, place the fillets on to warmed plates and top with a generous spoonful of the rocket sauce. Serve at once.

NOTE: The rocket sauce freezes very well.

Spaghetti with Goat's Cheese, Walnuts and Rocket

This delicious dish should be served in small quantities, for it is very rich. My recipe is based on a creation of one of the most famous Californian chefs, Alice Waters. Her dish incorporates rocket and green beans into a creamy sauce, which is served with buckwheat pasta. I have added a coarse texture to the sauce, with the walnuts. I like to grind them only a little, so they do not become a cloying paste. By using the 'pulse' switch on your food processor, you should end up with crumbly, rough textured ground nut – ideal for this sauce. (If you have no food processor, use a pestle and mortar.) The type of goat's cheese you buy is crucial to the finished flavour. Use a mild, young cheese so the flavour is tangy and sharp, rather than a pungent, overpowering, mature one. (A rough guideline, if there is no expert cheesemonger to ask, is that many younger goat's cheeses will not have developed a rind.) In this recipe, the rocket is torn at the last minute and tossed into the pan; the heat of the spaghetti wilts the rocket, so both colour and flavour remain fresh. Serve this with a salad dressed in a light vinaigrette, perhaps made with sunflower oil, a little mustard and plenty of lemon juice. (serves 4–5)

½ pint/300 ml double cream
4 oz/125 g soft goat's cheese,
2 oz/50 g walnuts, roughly ground
12–14 oz/375-425 g spaghetti
1 oz/25 g butter, roughly cubed
2½ oz/65 g rocket leaves
salt, pepper

1. In a saucepan, bring the cream to the boil, then reduce the heat to simmer. Add the cheese and walnuts and simmer gently for 3–4 minutes, until the cheese has melted into the cream.

2. Meanwhile, cook the spaghetti, drain well and toss it with the butter. Roughly tear the rocket leaves in half and put them into the pan. Toss the pasta, butter and rocket well together.

3. Pour the creamy sauce over the spaghetti in the pan, combine well, season to taste (you will need lots of freshly ground pepper) and serve at once in warmed bowls.

NOTE: Do not freeze.

A Portable Picnic Loaf

This bread recipe is ideal for picnics. Never again will you resort to pre-packed quiche and sandwich spread. The wonderful thing about the recipe is that it is so versatile. Instead of salami, you can use ham or tuna; add some capers or anchovies; rub a cut clove of garlic into the bread before filling. You can even spread a thin layer of tapenade (black olive paste) on the inside of the lid, before sealing. The amount of olive oil seems rather excessive, but it all depends what size of loaf you use; spoon over just enough oil to seep in, without flooding the bread. As for the cheese, I prefer Mozzarella, but you could also use Feta. The peppery flavour of the rocket leaves completes this gastronomic assault on the taste buds. It is essential to prepare this the night before your picnic – it should be kept for at least 12 hours and up to 30 hours, before opening. Weight it down, once you have wrapped it, with cartons of orange juice or milk. You will need a very sharp knife to cut it, otherwise the delicious, moist filling will escape. (serves 6–8)

---

1 large country loaf (ciabatta is also good)
4–5 tablespoons extra-virgin olive oil
2–3 oz/50–75 g good salami (not the bright pink variety)
1 large red pepper, grilled until charred, skin removed and sliced
2-3 artichoke hearts (carciofini, marinated in oil), sliced
1–2 large (beef) tomatoes, thinly sliced
2 oz/50 g rocket leaves
salt, pepper
4–6 oz/125–175 g Mozzarella, cut into thin slices
12–16 black olives, pitted and sliced

---

1. Cut the bread in half, horizontally. Remove most of the soft bread inside, leaving room for the filling. (All you want are thickish crusts; freeze the bread you remove as breadcrumbs.)

2. Spoon 3–4 tablespoons of olive oil carefully into both sides of the bread, just enough to soak lightly into it. Pack in the salami, pepper, artichokes, tomatoes and rocket into one half. Season well with plenty of salt and pepper. Press down gently with the palm of your hand, then continue layering. Add the cheese, then the olives, then season a little more. Spoon over the remaining 1 tablespoon olive oil.

3. Replace the 'lid', then carefully press both sides together. Wrap tightly in double foil, then in clingfilm. (Be careful while wrapping that the filling does not come out.)

4. Place in the salad drawer of the fridge. Put a weight on top, and leave for a minimum of 12 hours, before unwrapping and slicing with a very sharp knife.

NOTE: Do not freeze.

Rocket and Smoked Ham Omelette

There is nothing more satisfying than a delicious omelette. And this is so simple. Although it can be served hot, I prefer serving it warm. You can even roll it up like a swiss roll, leave it to become quite cold and cut into neat slices, to serve as an unusual canapé, with drinks. If serving cold, you might want to increase the amount of mustard. If you use a non-stick omelette pan, you will need ¼ oz/7 g butter; for a regular pan, use ½ oz/15 g. (serves 1)

3 eggs
1 oz/25 g rocket leaves
½ teaspoon wholegrain mustard
salt, pepper
½ oz/15 g butter
1 thin slice smoked ham

1. Beat the eggs in a bowl, then coarsely chop the rocket leaves and add these, with the mustard to the bowl. Season well with salt and pepper and beat together thoroughly.

2. Melt the butter in an omelette pan until hot. Pour in the egg mixture and cook for 2–3 minutes, until nearly set. Then lay the slice of ham on one side and, using a large spatula, carefully fold over to enclose the ham.

3. Cook for a further 1–2 minutes, then serve hot, warm or cold.

NOTE: Do not freeze.

Crêpes with Rocket and Pine Kernels, in Tomato Sauce

These crêpes are filled with a succulent mixture of Ricotta, Parmesan, garlic, toasted pine kernels and rocket. They are placed in an ovenproof dish and topped with tomato sauce, then baked in the oven. To make the crêpes, use 4 oz/125 g plain flour, 1 egg, ½ pint/300 ml milk and a pinch of salt (see Dill Crêpes, page 54) This will yield about 10 crêpes, the leftovers will do for the children's tea with lemon or maple syrup. Make them in advance and stack on a plate (there is no need to layer greaseproof paper in between, unless you want to freeze them). The tomato sauce is simple: just bake good flavoured tomatoes (not the insipid greenhouse ones which taste only of water) with oil and a sprinkling of sugar, then whizz together to make a tasty tomato sauce; the sauce is also handy to toss into pasta, or serve with meatloaf or meat balls. (serves 6 as a starter; 3 as a main course)

Sauce	Crêpes
4 large tomatoes	6 crêpes (about 7 in/18 cm)
1 teaspoon sugar	1 oz/25 g butter
2 tablespoons extra-virgin olive oil	2 garlic cloves, peeled and finely chopped
salt, pepper	2 oz/50 g rocket, roughly chopped
	4 oz/125 g Ricotta cheese
	1 oz/25 g Parmesan, freshly grated
	1 oz/25 g pine kernels, toasted
	salt, pepper

1. For the sauce, preheat the oven to Gas Mark 6/200°C/400°F. Cut the tomatoes in half, then scoop out and discard the seeds (I find a grapefruit spoon is best for this). Place on an ovenproof dish, cut side up. Sprinkle the sugar over the top, then drizzle over the olive oil. Bake in the preheated oven for about 25 minutes until the tomatoes are tender.

2. Transfer the entire contents of the dish into a food processor and whizz until smooth. Season well with salt and pepper (you may like to add a little more sugar). Push through a sieve to eliminate skins, then check the seasoning and reserve.

3. Melt the butter in a pan, add the garlic and cook for 1 minute. Stir in the rocket and cook for no more than 1 minute. Remove from the heat.

4. Mix this mixture into a bowl with the Ricotta, Parmesan and pine kernels. Season well with salt and pepper.

5. Place a heaped dessertspoon of this mixture on to one side of each crêpe, and roll up, like sausage-rolls. Lay them in an ovenproof dish. Spoon over the sauce (I like to do this in lines up and down, rather than just tipping it all over). Depending on the type of tomato, the sauce might look rather liquid at this stage, but do not panic: after 30 minutes in the oven, it thickens up slightly. (At this stage, the crêpes can be kept in the fridge for up to 8 hours, then baked.)

6. Preheat the oven to Gas Mark 4/180°C/350°F. Bake the crêpes, uncovered, for 25–30 minutes until piping hot. Serve at once.

NOTE: The dish is better not frozen.

chapter 14

rosemary

Native to the Mediterranean, rosemary (*Rosmarinus officinalis*) is an evergreen shrub with a distinctive aromatic smell and warm, resinous flavour. There is an early Christian legend that the rosemary bush would only grow as tall as Christ when he was on earth: it is rare to see rosemary grow higher than 6 feet. The Romans introduced it to Britain, where it thrives best in light, sandy soils in a sheltered position. Its white, pink or blue flowers, which have a similar, but milder taste to the leaves, are not purely decorative: their culinary uses, although not as extensive as the leaves, are considerable.

Historically there have been many accounts of the medicinal and remedial powers of rosemary. In Ancient Greece students twined bands of rosemary around their heads to stimulate their memories during exams. In Elizabethan England infusions of rosemary were prescribed to counteract baldness. Nowadays, rosemary is used in aromatherapy to invigorate and stimulate circulation. The essential oil is also purported to ease fatigue and strengthen memory retention. It is used frequently to soothe away headaches and to aid digestion.

The digestive benefits explain why it is often used with fatty or rich meats such as lamb, pork, goose or duck. The classic dish of lamb with rosemary is one of the most popular methods of cooking lamb: a whole leg is pierced all over with the tip of a knife, then slivers of garlic and rosemary leaves inserted, before being roasted. Kid is often treated the same way in Italy and adding a few freshly chopped rosemary leaves to roast potatoes, moussaka, cottage pie or pot-roast chicken greatly enhances simple everyday fare.

Rosemary goes equally well with fish, rabbit and Mediterranean vegetables such as aubergines, tomatoes and courgettes. Its aromatic flavour also lends itself to breads, scones or biscuits. The delicate flowers can be folded into light fools and creams, either to stand on their own, or as accompaniments to pies, tarts or crumbles. To prepare the flowers, cut them with their stems on and place in a glass of water until ready to use. Then carefully pinch the flowers away from the stems, rinse only if necessary and pat dry. A rosemary-flavoured oil is handy to have in the kitchen and is easy to make. You can use it in bread dough or in marinades, or brush it on to meat, fish or vegetable before grilling, roasting or barbecuing.

It is important to use only the young, tender leaves where chopped rosemary is required, and even the most tender should be very finely chopped. Use the older, tougher leaves solely for flavour: add a whole sprig to bouquet garnis or the stock for sauces. In Provence, I have seen locals use straight rosemary branches (devoid of leaves and stems) as skewers for kebabs and barbecued meats and small stems of rosemary leaves dipped in olive oil to baste them.

Use rosemary with discretion, always tasting as you introduce it to a dish, for its strong flavour can easily dominate less robust ingredients. Although rosemary dries fairly well, there should be no excuse to use anything other than fresh all year; it is, after all, evergreen. The one caveat to note is the legend that it grows only in the gardens of the righteous.

Rosemary Olive Oil

It is essential to use a good quality oil for this. I always use an extra-virgin olive oil, which assimilates the strong flavour of the herb easily. Inferior oils are invariably drowned by the rosemary. It can be kept in a cool place for several months. Should it solidify, in colder winter months, bring it to room temperature for an hour before using. A similar oil can be made with thyme, basil, tarragon or bay. (makes 8 fl oz/250 ml)

5–6 thick sprigs rosemary (about 6 in/15 cm long)
8 fl oz/250 ml extra virgin olive oil
1 teaspoon white wine vinegar
1 sprig rosemary (to finish)

1. Clean and dry the rosemary sprigs. Place them in a bottle or jar and top up with the olive oil. Add the vinegar, screw on the top or lid firmly and place on a window sill.

2. Every time you pass, give the bottle or jar a good shake. Leave for 2 weeks (3 weeks in winter), then strain the oil into a clean bottle, pop in a fresh sprig of rosemary and screw on the top. Keep in a cool place.

Cod with Olive and Rosemary Paste

Once you have made the olive and rosemary paste, it will keep in the fridge for a couple of weeks. You can spread any leftovers in a thin layer on to bruschetta or toast, then top with goat's cheese or Feta. Stir some of the paste into a hearty lamb or rabbit casserole towards the end of cooking or add a spoonful to mayonnaise and serve with cold roast beef or chicken. You can use fresh tuna steaks as an alternative to the cod: alter cooking times according to the thickness and weight of the fish. Accompany this dish with sauté potatoes, braised lentils or ratatouille. Choose a hearty red wine to accompany the robust flavours. (serves 4)

Paste
4 oz/125 g black olives (preferably
   Kalamata)
1 large garlic clove, peeled and chopped
1 oz/25 g anchovy fillets, drained
2 tablespoons capers, drained
1 heaped tablespoon chopped
   rosemary leaves
salt, pepper

juice of ½ lemon
freshly ground black pepper
3½ –4 fl oz/100–125 ml extra-virgin
   olive oil
Cod
4 x 8–10 oz/250–300 g thick cod steaks
½ teaspoon Dijon mustard
rosemary oil or olive oil to brush
1 oz/25 g fresh breadcrumbs

1. Stone the olives and place in a food processor with the remaining paste ingredients, adding sufficient oil to make a thick but not runny paste. Taste and season – you will probably not need salt as anchovies are salty. Refrigerate for 30 minutes.

2. Preheat the grill to high. Place the steaks on an oiled grillproof plate, and brush them with some oil. Season lightly. Grill the fish for about 5 minutes on one side.

3. Then carefully turn them over. Spread over a layer of the paste (not too thick), then divide the breadcrumbs over the tops, pressing lightly. Grill for a further 3–5 minutes, or until the fish is just cooked. Test with the tip of a knife to see if the flesh is cooked through.

5. Serve hot with a little of the juices poured over. NOTE: The paste can be frozen but not the fish.

Rosemary and Tomato Bread

This moist bread should be served warm, without butter. The rosemary flavour comes from the topping of fresh leaves and also from rosemary oil in the dough. If you do not have any, use olive oil and increase the herbs in the topping. Use sun-dried tomatoes preserved in either pure olive oil or a blend of olive and sunflower oils. If you have never made bread before, you will see how simple it is with easy-blend dried yeast. If you prefer using fresh yeast, however, combine 1 oz/25 g with a little of the hand-hot water and a pinch of sugar, before mixing into the flour. (makes one large loaf)

1 teaspoon salt
1 lb/500 g strong white flour, sifted
1½ teaspoons easy-blend dried yeast
2 tablespoons rosemary oil
1 tablespoon oil from the jar of tomatoes
8–10 fl oz/250–300 ml hand-hot water
few sprigs of rosemary
1 tablespoon sun-dried tomatoes, drained and chopped
extra olive oil, to brush
coarse sea salt

1. Mix the salt, flour and yeast together. Add the rosemary oil and tomato oil and then sufficient hand-hot water to form a soft dough. Turn on to a floured board and knead for about 10 minutes, until it feels smooth.

2. Place in a lightly oiled bowl, cover with clingfilm and allow to rise for about 1½ hours in a warm place. (I use the airing cupboard.)

3. Remove the dough to the board, punch it down with your fists, then press it out onto a large oiled baking tin (a swiss-roll tin is good), to a thickness of about ½ in/1 cm. You can make the shape either oval or rectangular.

4. With your knuckles, mark out little dimples all over, then tuck a little piece of rosemary, or a sliver of sun-dried tomato into each dimple. Brush with olive oil, sprinkle lightly with sea salt and allow to rise again in the warmth for about 30 minutes.

5. Meanwhile, preheat the oven to Gas Mark 8/230°C/450°F. Bake the bread in the middle of the oven for 15–20 minutes, until it sounds hollow when tapped underneath.

6. Remove from the oven, brush with a little more oil and serve warm.

NOTE: The bread freezes well.

Chickpea and Rosemary Soup

This soup is similar to an Italian chickpea soup traditionally eaten on fast days, for example during Lent. It is in fact such a delicious, hearty soup that you will want to eat it all year round. Sometimes fresh lasagne is made, cut by hand and dropped into the soup to cook at the last minute. This is delicious, but I prefer some rosemary-flavoured croutons, to provide a good crunchy texture. I like to simply tear the bread roughly into pieces, rather than cutting into neat cubes: it is, after all, an unsophisticated peasant dish. The method of thickening — by puréeing a couple of ladlefuls, then returning to the soup — means you have a soup to suit everyone: chunky chickpeas in a smooth thick purée. It is not necessary to use stock; there is ample flavour from the chickpeas and rosemary. Make sure you use the fruitiest olive oil for drizzling over at the end; and do remember to start making the soup the night before. (serves 6)

1 lb/500 g dried chickpeas
3 tablespoons olive oil
1 large onion, peeled and chopped
2 sticks celery, chopped
2 large sprigs of rosemary
2 large garlic cloves, peeled and crushed
salt, pepper
extra-virgin olive oil (to serve)

Croûtons
2 slices thick (Italian) bread, cubed or torn into croûtons
2–3 tablespoons extra-virgin olive oil
1 rosemary sprig

1. Rinse the chickpeas and soak in water overnight. Next day, place the peas into a large saucepan. Cover with enough of the soaking liquor to cover by about 1½ in/4 cm. Bring to the boil, then remove any scum with a slotted spoon.

2. Meanwhile, heat 3 tablespoons oil in a frying pan and gently fry the onion and rosemary sprigs (keep them whole; they will be removed later) for about 5 minutes, then add the celery and garlic. Cook gently for another 5 minutes.

3. Add the contents of the frying pan to the chickpeas, cover and simmer for about 3 hours.

4. Remove the herb sprigs (don't worry if some of the leaves have fallen off). Put 4 ladlefuls of the soup into the blender or food processor and purée, then return to the pan. Season well with salt and pepper. (I add a good 2 teaspoons salt, but taste and decide yourself.) Cook for another 5 minutes while you make the croûtons.

5. Heat the extra-virgin olive oil until hot, then add the bread and rosemary. Fry until golden. Remove the bread on to kitchen paper to drain.

6. To serve, ladle the soup into bowls, top with the croûtons, then drizzle over some fruity olive oil at the very last minute.

NOTE: The soup freezes well. The croûtons should not be frozen.

Black Pudding with Apples and Rosemary

This aromatic variation of the classic French 'boudin aux pommes' is simple but very effective. The flavour from the rosemary comes from lightly cooking the butter with rosemary sprigs for about 5 minutes. During this time, keep pressing down the herbs to release the flavour into the butter. This then flavours the black pudding and apples. Make sure your black pudding is top quality: your butcher's own pudding, made in natural casing should be the best. My butcher spices his generously with Jamaican pepper, so no seasoning is required once cooked. You may want to add pepper if the pudding is blander. (serves 4)

1 large ring of black pudding
3 oz/75 g unsalted butter
4 large sprigs of rosemary
4 dessert apples, preferably Cox's, peeled, cored and thickly sliced
rosemary to decorate

1. Cut the black pudding into 4 pieces and prick all over.
2. Melt the butter over a gentle heat and add the rosemary. Cook the butter for about 5 minutes, pressing the herbs down with a wooden spoon.
3. Add the apple slices and fry for about 3 minutes, until just tender. Remove them with a slotted spoon and keep warm.
4. Add the black pudding and fry for about 6–8 minutes, turning in the herb-flavoured butter.
5. Serve the black pudding on warmed plates, topped with apple slices. Strain over a little of the butter from the pan and decorate with fresh rosemary.

NOTE: Do not freeze.

Mushrooms with Garlic and Rosemary

This starter (or vegetarian main course) requires lots of crusty bread to mop up the rosemary and garlic-flavoured juices. You can vary the recipe by sprinkling over some fresh breadcrumbs, grated Parmesan cheese or chopped anchovies before baking. The lime adds an essential sharp edge to the dish. If you prefer using lemon, use the juice of a whole lemon. (serves 4)

4 large field mushrooms, wiped clean
3 garlic cloves, peeled and finely chopped
1 tablespoon freshly chopped rosemary
4 tablespoons extra virgin olive oil or rosemary oil
salt, pepper
the juice of ½ lime

1. Preheat the oven to Gas Mark 6/200°C/400°F.
2. Remove the stalks from the mushrooms and place in an oiled ovenproof dish. Sprinkle the garlic and rosemary over the mushrooms, then drizzle over the oil. Season with salt and freshly ground pepper, then bake in the oven for 15–20 minutes until tender.
3. Remove from the oven, squeeze over the lime juice and serve piping hot, with plenty of crusty bread to dunk into the oily juices.

NOTE: Do not freeze.

Oatmeal Tart with Aubergine, Tomato and Rosemary

A crisp oatmeal pastry is the base for aubergines, tomatoes and rosemary in this tart. A thick tomato sauce adds extra moisture and grated cheese forms an appetising golden crust. This is an ideal lunch or supper dish, served with a green salad, dressed with hazelnut or walnut oil and raspberry vinegar. Use this wonderful pastry for other tarts, as a base for smoked fish, spinach or bacon fillings. (serves 6)

Pastry	Filling
6 oz/175 g plain flour, sifted	1 large aubergine
3 oz/75 g medium oatmeal	salt
¾ teaspoon salt	2 garlic cloves, peeled and chopped
5 oz/150 g unsalted butter, cubed	3 tablespoons olive oil
1 egg	8 oz/250 g tin chopped tomatoes
1 tablespoon olive oil	1 tablespoon freshly chopped rosemary leaves
	2 extra-large tomatoes, sliced
	1½ oz/40 g mature Cheddar, grated
	1 sprig rosemary, chopped

1. For the pastry, place the flour, oatmeal and salt in a food processor. Add the butter and process until it resembles breadcrumbs. Mix the egg and oil, then add the mixture through the feeder tube. Process briefly and then bring together with your hands. (If you have no food processor, simply make the pastry by hand.) Wrap in clingfilm and chill for 30 minutes.

2. Slice the aubergines and salt them generously. Leave for 1 hour, to draw out the juices.

3. Fry the garlic in ½ tablespoon oil until golden, then add the tinned tomatoes and the rosemary. Cook uncovered for about 10 minutes, until thick. Season to taste.

4. Using kitchen paper, wipe the aubergines dry. Fry them in the remaining 2½ tablespoons oil until tender. Drain on kitchen paper.

5. Roll out the pastry to fit a 9 in/23 cm tart tin, prick all over and chill for at least 30 minutes. Preheat the oven to Gas Mark 5/190°C/375°F. Bake the tart blind, with foil and baking beans, for 15 minutes. Then remove the foil and beans and cook for a further 5 minutes.

6. Cool the pastry slightly, then arrange the aubergines on the base. Top with tomato sauce, then the fresh tomato slices. Sprinkle the cheese and rosemary over the top. Bake in the oven for 20–25 minutes, until the cheese has melted. Leave for 15 minutes and serve warm with a salad.

NOTE: Do not freeze.

Blueberry and Rosemary Cake

It is rare to find rosemary in sweet dishes. The addition of both rosemary oil and some finely chopped fresh leaves to this blueberry cake, however, is both unusual and exquisite. If you have no rosemary oil, simply substitute sunflower oil, but add extra rosemary to the topping. The texture of the cake is wonderfully crunchy because of the polenta. The topping is crumbly. Serve the cake warm, either with sweetened cream or Mascarpone; mix 1 tablespoon caster sugar to every 4 tablespoons Mascarpone cream cheese. For added flavour, fold in a handful of rosemary flowers to the cream or Mascarpone just before serving. (serves 8)

6 oz/175 g plain flour, sifted
pinch of salt
3 oz/75 g fine polenta
1 teaspoon baking powder
4 oz/125 g golden caster sugar
grated zest of 1 small orange
4 oz/125 g unsalted butter, cubed
1 large egg
1 tablespoon rosemary oil

Filling
12 oz/375 g blueberries
1 oz/25 g demerara sugar
2 teaspoons polenta

Topping
1 heaped teaspoon very finely chopped young rosemary leaves
1 level tablespoon demerara sugar

1. Place the flour, salt, polenta, baking powder and golden caster sugar in a food processor with the orange zest. Process briefly, then add the butter and process until it resembles breadcrumbs. Mix the egg and oil and add through the feeder tube.
2. Preheat the oven to Gas Mark 4/180°C/350°F. Press half the dough into a deep, buttered, 9 in/23 cm tart or cake tin, levelling off with the back of a spoon.
3. Mix the filling ingredients together and pile on to the base, taking care to leave about ½ in/1 cm around the edge. Sprinkle over the remaining dough as if it were a crumble mixture.
4. Mix the topping ingredients together and sprinkle over the top. Bake in the oven for about 50 minutes, until golden brown. Allow to cool for at least 20 minutes, before serving warm with sweetened cream or Mascarpone cheese.

NOTE: The cake freezes very well.

chapter 15

sage

Garden sage (*Salvia officinalis*) is a hardy evergreen shrub, which can grow in most soil types, although it prefers a well-drained soil and sunny location. It is a perennial, with pale grey-green leaves and purplish-blue flower spikes, and can be grown either from seed or from cuttings. There are a number of different varieties, but for cooking purposes the narrow-leaved or broad-leaved are best. There is golden sage (*Salvia officinalis Icterina*), which has fairly narrow leaves with a beautiful golden-green tinge to them; also purple or red sage (*Salvia officinalis Purpurascens*): both are good for cooking and make splendid garnishes. Garden sage is native to the northern Mediterranean, from Spain to the Adriatic. In a reversal of usual roles, sage was introduced from Europe into China, where sage tea became very popular; so popular indeed that they traded their own world-famous tea in exchange for it. Sage tea is an excellent tonic for those with nervous complaints and is recommended as a remedy for rheumatic pain and for anaemia. In aromatherapy, the oil of clary sage (*Salvia sclarea*), which is not used in cooking nowadays, is used to treat mental fatigue, anxiety and depression.

In former times, sage was prescribed to treat almost every ailment imaginable. (It is worth noting that the etymology of the genus comes from the Latin 'salvare', to save; hence its multifarious health-keeping qualities!) The Greeks used it as remedy for most kidney disorders and also for ulcers and consumption. In Roman times, it was not only considered a sacred herb, but recommended to women who had difficulty in becoming pregnant. Some centuries later in this country, Samuel Pepys recorded in his diary how sage was customarily grown on graves, for it was believed that the herb alleviated grief. Gargles made with sage were administered for coughs and sore throats.

Sage has a powerful and distinctive flavour, which has overtones of camphor. It is a versatile herb to cook with but it should be used in cautious quantity, for its strong taste may completely overpower other flavours. When grown in hot, dry climates, it is even stronger. The old English favourite, sage and onion stuffing, is an ideal example of when it is best used: it is first combined with equally pungent onions; then used to stuff strong-flavoured meats like goose, pork or duck. (Remember the Beatrix Potter tale: 'Jemima Puddleduck was a simpleton; not even the mention of sage and onions made her suspicious'.) Sage works well with fatty foods, such as sausages, and oily fish, because it aids the digestion of them. In Germany and Belgium, eels are often cooked with sage. In Italy, sage is a vital ingredient of the classic 'saltimbocca', in which flattened veal escalopes are topped with a whole sage leaf, a slice of ham and sometimes cheese, then rolled tightly, fried in butter and finished with a marsala sauce. Whole sage leaves can also be used at barbecues, threaded between chunks of meat or fish in kebabs. One of the least subtle of herbs, it has the ability to transform the simplest of dishes into something more aromatic and sophisticated; for example, the lowly hamburger becomes a gastronomic treat by adding some freshly chopped sage.

Deep-fried Sage Leaves with Roasted Garlic Aioli

The roasted garlic mayonnaise for this recipe is also delicious with chips. The concept of frying whole herb leaves is perhaps new to some, but it is well worth having a go at. Start off with sage (I like to use broad-leaved or red sage for this), then experiment with basil and of course parsley, which makes the most perfect accompaniment to fried fish. The leaves should be fairly large, completely dry and clean. Only fry them for a short time and watch they do not burn. They can be fried in advance and reheated in a medium oven for about 5 minutes, just before serving. Serve as a starter, or as a pre-prandial appetiser. (serves 4)

20–24 large sage leaves	Aioli
oil, for deep-fat frying	6 large (8 small) garlic cloves, unpeeled
	salt
	1 egg
	4 fl oz/125 ml sunflower oil
	1 tablespoon freshly squeezed lemon juice
	approximately 3 fl oz/90 ml olive oil
	pepper

1. Heat the fat in a deep-fat fryer to about 180°C/350°F. Then drop the sage leaves in and fry for about 40–60 seconds. Drain on kitchen paper. Keep warm if serving immediately.

2. For the aioli, preheat the oven to Gas Mark 4/180°C/350°F. Place the garlic cloves on a lightly-oiled baking tray and bake for 20–25 minutes, until you can feel the inside is soft and pulpy. Remove and allow to cool sufficiently to handle. Then snip the top off each clove and, as if you were squeezing toothpaste, squeeze out the pulp into a food processor. Add salt to taste and the egg. Process for about 30 seconds, then add the lemon juice and process for a couple of seconds, until it is well-blended. Then, very slowly, pour in the sunflower oil, drop by drop at first, steadily allowing it to become a thin steady stream. Continue with the olive oil, using just enough to form the consistency of thinnish mayonnaise (not too thick like a dip). Add seasoning to taste and place in a bowl. If time permits, chill for an hour or so.

3. Serve the hot sage leaves in a bowl and invite guests to dip them into a bowl of mayonnaise. NOTE: Do not freeze.

Orange Roast Potatoes

The potatoes in this recipe are roasted in a mixture of orange and sage. They should be basted with the oil often so they become very crunchy on the outside. Their tangy citrus flavour makes them an ideal accompaniment to a joint of pork, beef or veal; or to grilled salmon or lamb chops. Be sure to cut the potatoes into fairly small dice, so they are well-cooked. A rough guide is around 14–16 cubes per large potato. (serves 4)

3 tablespoons olive oil	3 large potatoes, peeled and
the zest of 1 orange	cut into dice
4–6 sage leaves, roughly chopped	salt, pepper

1. Preheat the oven to Gas Mark 7/220°C/425°F. Place the oil, orange zest and sage in a roasting tin and place in a preheated oven for 5 minutes.

2. Dry the potatoes well on a clean tea-towel, then tip them into the roasting tin. Toss around, to coat with the oil and season well with salt and pepper. Place in the oven and roast for 40–45 minutes, basting often, until golden brown and cooked through. NOTE: Do not freeze.

Roast Red Onions

These onions become caramelised and golden as they bake in a mixture of olive oil and balsamic vinegar. The onions are good at an informal supper or lazy summer lunch, or even as accompaniment to barbecue food such as kebabs or burgers. They can also become part of a mixed platter of hors d'oeuvres, which might include grilled peppers and aubergines, black olives or wild mushrooms preserved in oil. In this case, serve with plenty of fresh crusty bread. For colour and taste, the onions are also the perfect companions to simply fried or grilled steak. (serves 4)

4 large red onions	1 tablespoon sage leaves, finely
4 tablespoons olive oil	chopped
2 tablespoons balsamic vinegar	salt, pepper

1. Preheat the oven to Gas Mark 7/220°C/425°F. Slice the tops off the onion, then peel. It is important as you do this to keep the root end intact, or the onion layers will all separate. Place on a chopping board, cut-side up, and cut into half, then into quarters.

2. Place them in a roasting tin. Pour over the oil and vinegar, then sprinkle over the sage leaves. Season well with salt and pepper. Toss well, so they are all coated, and cover loosely with foil. Place in the preheated oven for about 45 minutes, then remove the foil and cook for a further 10 minutes, until they are soft and caramelised. Serve at once. NOTE: Do not freeze.

Veal with Mustard and Sage Sauce

I do not eat veal, so I suggest using pork chops as an alternative; sage goes very well with both veal and pork. The sauce can also be used to accompany a roast joint of meat; simply make it in the baking tin (directly on the heat) while the roast rests. If you are frying the meat, go for either escalopes or loin chops. A couple of deep-fried sage leaves (see page 128) would make the most wonderfully crunchy garnish. Serve with buttered noodles or rice and a fresh green vegetable, such as spinach. (serves 4)

1 oz/25 g butter	2 teaspoons Dijon mustard
1 tablespoon olive oil	2 tablespoons crème fraîche
4 veal escalopes or pork chops	4–6 sage leaves, finely chopped
3–4 shallots, peeled and finely chopped	salt, pepper
2 tablespoons dry sherry	

1. Melt the butter and oil in a frying pan. When very hot, add the meat and brown on both sides. Then reduce the heat to medium and fry until cooked through. Remove and keep warm.

2. Increase the heat and add the shallots to the pan. Fry these gently for about 3 minutes, then increase the heat and add the sherry. Bubble for 1 minute, then add the mustard, stir, then add the crème fraîche and sage. Stir well. Cook over a fairly high heat for about 2 minutes again, stirring well. Season with salt and pepper, then serve with the meat. NOTE: Do not freeze.

Sage Jelly

This jelly recipe can be used with a variety of different herbs. Depending on their texture, they are either chopped finely and added to the jelly pan before potting, or a whole sprig of the herb is added after potting. Herbs which I suggest for the former are: parsley, mint and oregano. Those more suitable for the latter are rosemary and thyme. If you have never made jelly before, it is easy as long as you follow certain rules. First, you must leave the jelly bag dripping for a minimum of 12 hours; up to 24 hours, providing the weather is not tropical. Do not be tempted to squeeze or poke the jelly bag, or the finished jelly will be very cloudy. Only use cooking apples, which have a much higher pectin level than dessert ones. Windfalls are ideal for jellies, since after a quick wash and removal of any bruised parts, the whole apple is used – cores, skins and all. I prefer to use crab-apples, when possible. Some recipes for herb jellies advise adding a few drops of green food colouring, but I prefer not to – it is all too easy to overdo it and ruin the jelly. I suggest serving this sage jelly with roast pork or spread over veal or pork chops during grilling, or added to the pan juices as you make your gravy from roast pork. (makes 3–4 jars)

3 lb/1.25 kg cooking apples, washed	1 pint/600 ml distilled clear vinegar
1½ pints/900 ml water	granulated or preserving sugar
2 oz/50 g sage stalks and leaves	

1. Remove any damaged or bruised parts from the apples, then roughly chop them, cores and all, and put into a large jelly pan. Cover with the water, add all the sage stalks and half the leaves. Bring to the boil. Reduce to a simmer and cook for about 40 minutes, until soft and pulpy. Stir occasionally, pressing down on the herbs.

2. Meanwhile, prepare the apparatus for hanging the jelly bag. The bag will need to be suspended from either an upturned stool or a broom between 2 chairs with a bowl underneath it. Just before you are ready to pour the jelly mixture into the bag, scald the bag in boiling water.

3. Add the vinegar to the jelly mixture and bring to a rapid boil. Boil for 5 minutes. Remove and pour into the jelly bag. Leave to drip for 12–24 hours.

4. Discard the pulp and pour the contents of the bowl into a measuring jug. For every 1 pint/ 600 ml of liquid, add 1 lb/500 g granulated sugar. My amount works out to about 1¾ pints/ 1 litre, so use 1¾ lb/875 g of sugar. Heat very gently until the sugar is completely dissolved. Then bring slowly to the boil and allow to boil rapidly, stirring occasionally, for about 10 minutes until setting point is reached.

   I test by one of 3 methods. The most common one is to drop a little jelly on to a cold saucer. Once it has cooled slightly, push your finger through it. If the surface wrinkles, it is ready. (Remove the pan from the heat before testing, by the way.) Then, there is the flake test, which you can use once you feel more confident with the jelly-making procedure: lift your wooden spoon out of the jelly with some of the liquid on it. Keeping it high above the pan, allow it to drop back into the pan. If the last few drops run together, to form a long string, it is ready. Then there is my mother's method: again, hold the wooden spoon high above the pan. Once most of the liquid has dropped off, run the nail of your forefinger along the back of the spoon. If it leaves a discernible line which is fairly solid, then it is ready.

   Immediately setting point is reached, remove from the heat, discard any scum with a slotted spoon, and stir in the remaining sage leaves, which should be finely chopped.

5. Leave for a couple of minutes to cool slightly, then stir to distribute the sage and pot into warmed jars. (If you are using rosemary or thyme, then pot straight after setting point has been reached, and pop in a long sprig of the herb after half an hour or so.) Leave to become completely cold, then seal with a lid and label.

Sage and Cheese Burgers

These burgers are moist and succulent, with lots of flavour from the chopped sage. You can fry them, but I prefer them grilled; the cheese does not melt quite so seductively when fried. The cheesy filling is a wonderful surprise when you cut into the burger. You can substitute Mozzarella for the Gruyère if you prefer. These can also be cooked on a barbecue. (makes 4 large burgers)

1 lb/500 g lean minced beef	1 tablespoon Worcestershire sauce
3 shallots, finely chopped	salt, pepper
1 heaped tablespoon sage leaves, chopped	2 oz/50 g Gruyère, cut into 4 slices or 8 cubes
1 oz/25 g Parmesan, freshly grated	

1. Place the mince, shallots, sage, parmesan and Worcestershire sauce in a bowl. Season generously with salt and pepper. Mix everything together (I find using my hands is easiest).
2. Shape into 4 balls. Making a pocket in each, tuck in either 1 slice or 2 cubes of cheese. Remould into round flat shapes, ensuring all the cheese is covered by the meat. Set on a plate and refrigerate for at least 1 hour.
3. Preheat the grill. Place the burgers on a foil-lined grill tray and grill for about 4–5 minutes each side, or until done to your liking. NOTE: Without the cheese filling, the burgers can be frozen.

Bread Tartlets with Mushrooms and Sage

I never cease to be surprised how a mere ½ oz/15 g of dried wild mushrooms, such as ceps 'porcini' or morels can add so much flavour to a dish. You will notice the difference in this tasty starter which can also be served as a light lunch. Although I recommend using either shiitake, oyster or chestnut mushrooms, the ordinary button mushrooms will do, for there will be plenty of mushroom flavour from the dried ones. Sage and mushrooms blend very well together and a hint of garlic never goes amiss. To make the filling even richer, you can add 2 tablespoons of crème fraîche to the mushroom mixture at the very end, stir it in well. It is important not to season with salt at the end, just pepper, for most soy sauces are very salty. (serves 4)

Tartlets	Filling
8 slices wholemeal bread, crusts removed	½ oz/15 g dried ceps 'porcini', chopped
1½ oz/40 g butter, melted	2 tablespoons light soy sauce
	1 tablespoon hot water
	2 oz/50 g butter
	12 oz/375 g mixed mushrooms (such as shiitake, oyster, chestnut), chopped
	1 tablespoon sage, finely chopped
	2 garlic cloves, peeled and chopped
	pepper
	½ tablespoon lemon juice

1. Preheat the oven to Gas Mark 5/190°C/375°F. Use the melted butter to butter 8 shallow muffin or bun moulds; mine are about ¾ in/2 cm deep. Line each with a slice of unbuttered bread and place in the preheated oven for about 15–20 minutes, until crisp and golden.

2. Rinse, then soak the dried mushrooms in the soy sauce and hot water for at least 30 minutes. Then melt the butter and gently fry the mixed mushrooms, sage and garlic for 3 minutes. Add the soaked mushrooms and their soaking liquor, bring to the boil and bubble away for another 3 minutes, then season with pepper (not salt, as the soy sauce is salty) and reduce to a simmer. Cook for another 8–10 minutes, until all the mushrooms are cooked. Remove from the heat and stir in the lemon juice.

3. To serve, place 2 warm bread tartlets on a plate. Spoon the mushroom mixture into these and serve at once. NOTE: Do not freeze.

Caramelised Apple and Sage Tart with Wensleydale Cheese

This tart should be served at room temperature (but freshly baked if possible) with the thinnest of slices of Wensleydale cheese – or Cheddar is also good. The pastry for the tart is flavoured with sage, which works beautifully with the apples. I suggest using Granny Smiths, for their refreshingly tart flavour. Do not use cooking apples, which will not hold their shape. I use quince jelly for the caramelising, but you can use apple or sage jelly (see page 130) instead. If you are not keen on cheese, or are serving a cheese course, then serve the tart with some thick cream. Other herbs can be used in pastry to make sweet or savoury tarts (for savoury ones use a shortcrust pastry recipe). Especially to be recommended are parsley, thyme, oregano and marjoram.

Pastry	Filling
4 oz/125 g plain flour, sifted	2 oz/50 g unsalted butter
a pinch of salt	5 Granny Smiths (or 4 large), peeled,
2 oz/50 g caster sugar	cored and sliced
2 oz/50 g ground walnuts or almonds	juice of ½ lemon
1 heaped tablespoon sage leaves	2 tablespoons sugar
(about 10 leaves)	2 tablespoons quince or apple jelly
3 oz/75 g unsalted butter, cubed and	2 tablespoons water
chilled	To serve
1 egg yolk	4–5 thin slices of Wensleydale cheese
juice of ½ lemon	per person

1. For the pastry, place the flour, salt, sugar, ground nuts and sage into a food processor and process until combined. Add the cold butter and process until it resembles breadcrumbs. Add the egg yolk and lemon juice and process, then combine together with your hands into a ball, wrap in clingfilm and chill for at least 30 minutes. Roll out to fit a 8 in/20 cm metal tart tin. Prick with a fork and chill for at least 1 hour, preferably 2 hours or overnight.

2. Preheat the oven to Gas Mark 5/190°C/375°F. Bake the tart blind (with foil and baking beans) in the preheated oven for about 20 minutes. Then remove the foil and beans and cook for a further 5–10 minutes, until just cooked through. Lower the oven to Gas 4/180°C/ 350°F.

3. For the filling, melt the butter in a heavy-based pan, add the apples, lemon juice, jelly, sugar and water. Cook gently for about 2 minutes, until the sugar has melted. Increase the heat to high and cook for about 8 minutes, stirring occasionally, until caramelised and the apples are tender.

4. Tip the apple mixture into the tart case and return to the oven for a further 10 minutes, until just set.

5. Cool to serve at room temperature, topped with thin slices of cheese. NOTE: Do not freeze.

chapter 16

savory

Regrettably, savory is not a well-known herb in many kitchens. By means of introduction, therefore, I should explain that there are several species of the same genus. The two most common forms for cooking, however, are winter savory (*Satureia montana*) and summer savory (*Satureia hortensis*). Winter savory is a shrubby perennial with purplish flowers and thin green leaves, reminiscent of a softer-leaved rosemary. It is a woody plant and can be grown in poor soil and without much sun. Its flavour is not quite as fragrant as summer savory and is generally considered inferior, but it does have the advantage of being available for most of the year. Summer savory is a hardy annual, with long narrow leaves and small dainty lilac and pink flowers. Its flavour is more subtle, although more peppery and slightly spicier than winter savory; it has been described as similar to thyme, but with a more bitter taste. In terms of flavour, it is at its best just before it is in flower. Both savories have a strong taste and should be used judiciously.

The savories were recorded by Virgil, who classed them among the sweetest herbs; he advised planting them near bee-hives, to give an attractive taste to the honey. The Romans used it extensively in their cooking. They prepared a vinegar-based sauce from it, as a relish to accompany lamb, just like mint sauce. It was also added to stuffings for poultry and a flavouring for pies, sausages, eggs and meat.

Although both winter and summer savory can be used for similar types of recipes, you should be careful with amounts. In my recipes, I have stipulated which type I use. If you must use winter instead of summer savory (for example when it is out of season), then you might have to vary the amount needed, as the result will be less delicate than if you had used summer savory. But, as ever, taste as you add and adjust accordingly. Be careful; savory is a herb which can easily dominate every other ingredient.

Both types have been used medicinally over the centuries. They have been recommended to aid digestion and to relieve wind, flatulence, colic and nausea. Savory was also made into syrups, which were given as expectorants to relieve blocked-up chests, and also to alleviate asthmatic problems. It is also reputed to help provide relief from bee stings.

In cooking, both savories go well with beans, peas and lentils. They are excellent as flavourings in sausages and also in stuffings, for example for game or poultry. Winter savory has also been used in the past as a stuffing for trout. Savory is particularly popular as the herb to flavour pulses in Switzerland, Germany and France. Use savory in stews, or in soups, particularly in split pea soups. It also enhances good old-fashioned pease puddings and real home-made baked beans. Most meat dishes – for example pork, veal, duck and all sorts of charcuterie – benefit from the addition of a little savory. Hopefully, once you have tried my recipes with savory you will begin to appreciate its strong, spicy and aromatic taste. Then, experiment with other recipes – I believe this is a herb with potential!

Pea and Savory Soup

Although I would recommend using fresh garden peas for this, it can be made in winter, with frozen peas. However, the flavour is weaker with frozen peas and the colour more dull. If you do want to make this in winter, then substitute frozen peas for the fresh, but reduce the liquid to 1 pint/600 ml, otherwise, it will be too watery. I have used summer savory for this, but if you make it with frozen peas in winter, use winter savory, adjusting the amount according to taste. I had originally decided to reheat this soup with a carton of double cream and, indeed, this is still an optional extra. But I would suggest tasting it first, for I think the texture is already wonderfully creamy once you have sieved it. A compromise might be to swirl with a little double cream just before serving. The addition of some pea pods might seem rather strange, but in fact they add a delightful sweetness to the fresh pea soup. (serves 3)

2 oz/50 g butter	1¼ pint/750 ml water
1 onion, peeled and chopped	1 tablespoon summer savory, chopped
1 lb/500 g fresh peas (shelled weight)	salt, pepper
12 pea pods, topped and tailed	small carton of double cream, (optional)

1. Melt the butter and sauté the onion for about 10 minutes, until soft.

2. Add the peas and pea pods, stir well, then pour in the water and the savory and bring to the boil. Cover, reduce to a simmer and cook for about 10–15 minutes until the peas are just tender (not too long, or the bright colour will disappear).

3. Tip everything into a liquidiser and blend until smooth. Then push through a fine sieve, to eliminate all those stringy bits from the pods. Taste for seasoning and add salt and pepper. Reheat, then serve, with or without cream. If you add the cream, stir it in, then reheat together, but do not boil.

NOTE: The soup can be frozen without the cream; it will taste just as good, but will lose its fresh bright colour.

Oatmeal Fried Tomatoes

I love these oatmeal-covered tomatoes, which are fried to a crusty, golden finish, then served piping hot. They can either stand on their own as a light lunch, with plenty of good, warmed bread, or can be served as accompaniment to roast or grilled meat, such as lamb or beef. They are easy to prepare: you simply mix the oatmeal (it must be medium oatmeal, not oatflakes or jumbo oats) with grated Parmesan and some freshly chopped savory. This is then pressed into the cut tomatoes and they are fried until golden brown. Be sure to use firm yet ripe tomatoes. They should be neither too squashy, nor too hard. This dish exemplifies best of all how well just a little bit of savory (I use summer savory for this) enhances the flavour of simple, yet delicious dishes. (serves 4)

4 large tomatoes
2 oz/50 g Parmesan, freshly grated
2 oz/50 g medium oatmeal
salt, pepper
1 tablespoon summer savory, finely chopped
3 tablespoons olive oil

1. Cut the tomatoes into fairly thick slices and pat dry with kitchen paper.
2. Mix the Parmesan, oatmeal, salt, pepper and savory together in a bowl.
3. Press each tomato slice into the mixture until well coated.
4. Heat the oil in a large frying pan, then fry the tomato slices for about 2 minutes, until golden brown. Serve at once.

NOTE: Do not freeze.

Piperade

The full title should, of course, be Piperade Basquaise, for this tasty dish is from the Pays Basque area of France. But my version is perhaps not wholly authentic, firstly because of the addition of the savory (I used summer savory, for the vegetables in the recipe are cheapest and best in summer), and secondly because of the way the eggs are cooked. Herb-wise, it should be a little thyme, instead of the savory, but I think the flavour of savory works very well. When I ate this one a summer as an au pair in Provence, Madame threw in whatever was in the garden, usually thyme, but it might have been some freshly chopped parsley or even basil. Also, she never peeled the peppers; the only time this was done was when they were having 'grillades' (France's answer to Australia's 'barbie' or America's 'cook-out') and they would char-grill the peppers over the fire, before peeling and tossing them into a memorable salad, with olive oil and a few black olives. I happen to dislike unpeeled peppers in dishes, so whenever I can, I peel them. I also like the almost smoky effect resulting from grilling them. Finally, those eggs: Madame (who was a wonderful cook) always fried them in the piperade, never scrambled them. Many piperades, however, are more like scrambled eggs with peppers. This is also very good, but the consistency is different. Try both ways – they are equally delicious. (serves 3)

3 red peppers
1 tablespoon olive oil
4 oz/125 g smoked streaky bacon
1 large onion, peeled and chopped
3 garlic cloves, peeled and finely chopped
2 large tomatoes, chopped
1 heaped tablespoon summer savory, chopped
salt, pepper
3 eggs

1. Quarter the peppers, remove the seeds and place on foil under a hot grill until blackened. Remove and cover with the foil. Leave for about 20 minutes, or until cool enough to handle, then skin them and cut into dice.
2. Heat the oil in a large, heavy-based frying pan. Fry the bacon for 2 minutes, then add the onion and garlic and fry for 5 minutes.
3. Add the peppers and tomatoes, then stir in the savory. Over a medium heat, cook for about 15 minutes, stirring occasionally.
4. Add salt and pepper, then drop in 3 eggs and either allow them to fry where they are or, using a wooden spoon, scramble them into the pepper mixture. For fried eggs you will need about 5 minutes; for scrambled eggs about 3 minutes.
5. Taste again for seasoning and serve hot.

NOTE: Do not freeze.

Broccoli and Chilli Spaghetti

This is a variation on a couple of Italian dishes, one with olive oil and garlic, the other with broccoli and chilli. I suggest using a half of a normal-sized chilli, but a quarter of a large one will suffice. Once you have decided just how much chilli to use, then decide on the olive oil. Apart from the savory, the oil is one of the main flavourings. I suggest a fruity oil, which will balance well with the chilli. This is very much a last-minute dish, so have everything ready in advance, just to be tossed at the very end. Serve with a tomato salad and some fresh, warmed bread. (serves 4)

12 oz/375 g dried spaghetti	¼–½ dried chilli, finely chopped
12 oz/375 g broccoli florets	1 heaped tablespoon summer savory
5 tablespoons extra-virgin olive oil	salt, pepper
3 large garlic cloves, finely chopped	

1. Cook the spaghetti until *al dente*, then drain.
2. Meanwhile, cook the broccoli in boiling salted water for about 3–4 minutes, until just done. Drain well.
3. Heat the oil, then add the garlic and chilli and sauté gently for about 2 minutes. Do not allow the garlic to become too brown, or it will taste burnt.
4. Toss the flavoured oil with the garlic and chilli into the pasta, add the savory and salt and pepper and then the broccoli.
5. Toss well together and serve at once. NOTE: Do not freeze.

Savory Cornbread

This bread is slightly sweet, but mainly savoury (and also savory!). Its texture is not so much bread-like as cake-like. The polenta (cornmeal) gives it a rather coarse texture and wonderful golden yellow colour. The savory flavour comes through well, whether you decide to serve the bread warm or cold. For a real treat you can top it with a sliver of mature Cheddar. Serve it with a hearty soup, for lunch, or as a starter course, with an interesting salad and a glass of light red wine. (makes 1 cornbread)

8 oz/250 g plain flour	8 fl oz/250 ml milk
3 teaspoons baking powder	3 oz/75 g butter, melted
5 oz/150 g polenta	2 eggs
1 teaspoon salt	2 oz/50 g sugar
2 tablespoons summer savory	

1. Preheat the oven to Gas 7/220°C/425°F. Sift together the flour and baking powder in a bowl, and add the polenta, salt and savory.
2. Mix the milk and melted butter, then stir into the flour mixture.
3. Beat the eggs and sugar together and add to the bowl. Stir well (do not beat too much) and pour into a buttered, square tin, 8 in/20 cm.
4. Bake in the preheated oven for about 30 minutes, until well-risen and golden brown. Leave to cool for at least 5 minutes, then turn out on to a wire rack to cool. NOTE: Freezes well.

Sausages and Beans

Sausages and beans are everybody's favourite dish; children love baked beans and their favourite bangers and adults also love beans and sausages, if perhaps with more sophisticated flavours. To make tinned baked beans more 'grown-up', add a small glass of red wine while reheating them: beans on toast will never be the same again! For this recipe, I suggest using Lincolnshire sausages, which are flavoured mainly with sage, but other herby sausages would fit the bill. The beans are cooked, then mixed with a simple tomato sauce. Although I prefer using cannellini beans, haricot are also good. For this recipe, I used winter savory, for it is a hearty, cold weather dish, but do try it with summer savory, tasting as you add. (serves 6–8)

Beans	Sauce
1 lb/500 g dried beans	2 tablespoons olive oil
2 onions, peeled and chopped	1 large onion, peeled and chopped
2 garlic cloves, peeled and chopped	3 garlic cloves, peeled and chopped
2 tablespoons winter savory, chopped	2 x 13 oz/400 g tins of tomatoes,
salt, pepper	with their juices
	1 tablespoon winter savory, chopped
Sausages	1 heaped tablespoon tomato purée
2 lb/1 kg herby sausages	salt, pepper

1. Rinse, then soak the beans overnight. Drain, then cover with cold water. Add the onions, garlic and savory. Bring to the boil, then reduce to a simmer and cook, covered, for about 45–55 minutes, until tender. Drain the beans, reserving the liquid. Season them with plenty of salt and pepper.

2. For the sauce, heat the oil, and fry the onion and garlic for 2 minutes, then add the tomatoes and bring to the boil. Reduce the heat and cook, uncovered, for about 15–20 minutes, until they are slightly thickened. Then, using a potato masher, mash the tomato mixture, then add the savory, tomato purée and salt and pepper.

3. Meanwhile, grill the sausages until cooked.

4. Add the beans to the tomato sauce, stir well and add some of the cooking liquid if you think it is too thick. Reheat gently and taste for seasoning.

5. To serve, spoon the beans into a large serving dish and place the sausages on top.

NOTE: Do not freeze.

Lentils with Fried Eggs

Ever since I can remember, I have always loved lentils. We had plenty of lentil soup as children. Of course, it was always the bright orange lentils, which still make the most wonderful soup, with lots of root vegetables and some fresh thyme or savory. They turn to mush easily, which is just what is required for soup. But the lentils for this recipe – Puy lentils – hold their shape well, so are perfect for braising or salads. They are cooked until tender, then mixed with some melted butter, oil and savory, and served in a mound topped with a fried egg, Parmesan shavings and truffle oil. The latter is entirely optional, for I know its strong flavour is not everyone's favourite, but give it a try. Despite its astronomical price, you only require 1–2 drops, so it is in fact rather a bargain! To make Parmesan shavings, I use a swivel-headed potato peeler, and shave from a large block of Parmigiano Reggiano. This dish is so simple, yet unbelievably tasty. (serves 4)

8 oz/250 g Puy lentils	salt, pepper
3 tablespoons winter savory, chopped	4 small eggs
2 oz/50 g butter, melted	Parmesan shavings (to serve)
1 tablespoon olive oil	truffle oil (optional)

1. Rinse the lentils well, then place in a saucepan and cover with cold water. Add 2 tablespoons of the savory and bring to the boil. Boil rapidly for about 10 minutes, then reduce the heat and cover. Cook for a further 25 minutes, or until they are just tender.

2. Drain them if necessary. Then add 1½ oz/40 g melted butter and the oil. Stir well, adding the remaining savory and salt and pepper.

3. Meanwhile, heat the remaining butter in a frying pan and fry the eggs.

4. To serve, spoon a mound of lentils in four soup plates. Top each with a fried egg, then with some Parmesan shavings and a drop or two of truffle oil.

NOTE: Do not freeze.

Savory chicken

It is important to use a chicken with flavour for this; either a free-range one or a golden-yellow corn-fed one. The preparation method is perhaps slightly unusual, but the end result is the most succulent flesh with bags of flavour. So often roast chicken can be dry, but by this method you get a moist roast every time. Loosen the skin over the breast gently, to avoid tearing the skin, then smear in half of the savory dressing. The easiest way is to tip the chicken up towards you slightly, so you can slowly pour the mixture down each side of the breast, then place it back down and ease the mixture over both breasts. The fact that this wonderfully oily mixture is directly under the skin means that the flesh keeps moist and succulent and the taste of the savory permeates the entire dish. Although I like the chicken to be eaten at room temperature or, even better, at picnic temperature, it can also be served warm, once it has rested for about 30 minutes. I use summer savory for this recipe. (serves 4–6)

1 3lb/1.25 kg chicken	2 teaspoons Dijon mustard
salt, pepper	1 tablespoon white wine vinegar
1 small onion, peeled and quartered	4 tablespoons extra-virgin olive oil
½ lemon, quartered	2 tablespoons summer savory, chopped

1. Preheat the oven to Gas Mark 5/190°C/375°F. Place the chicken in a roasting tin. Season the insides with salt and pepper and tuck the onion and lemon quarters into the cavity.

2. In a screw-top jar, shake together the mustard, vinegar, oil, savory and salt and pepper. Once it has amalgamated well, carefully slide your hand between the chicken skin and the breast meat. Gently spread about half of this savory dressing over the breast meat. Then pour the remaining dressing over the whole bird. Place in the preheated oven for 20 minutes, then reduce the temperature to Gas Mark 4/180°C/350°F.

3. Basting with the savory dressing every 10–15 minutes, roast for a further 55–60 minutes, until the chicken is cooked (pierce the leg with a sharp knife; the juices should run clear).

4. Allow the chicken to rest for at least 30 minutes, or let it cool down sufficiently to pack in the picnic hamper, with a sharp knife, to cut *in situ*. Don't forget plenty of fresh bread to dunk into those oily juices.

NOTE: Do not freeze.

chapter 17

sorrel

Common (or garden) sorrel (*Rumex acetosa*) is a form of sour dock, closely related to rhubarb. The name, sorrel, originates from the Teutonic word for 'sour'. It is a perennial, native to Europe and Asia, and now also found wild in North America. Although the basic flavour is acidic and bitter, the varieties do differ. Common sorrel grows wild in grassland and meadows. It is also incredibly easy to grow in your garden. The first tender young leaves are the ones to serve raw in salads. The older, slightly tough ones should be used in soups and other cooked dishes. By staggering the times you sow your sorrel, you can be assured of both tender young leaves and the older, darker green ones too. Another variety of sorrel, called French or buckler-leaved sorrel (*Rumex scutatus*), is smaller in size and has leaves which are rounder and more reminiscent of tiny arrow-heads than the longer, broader, spear-shaped leaves of common sorrel. French sorrel is slightly less acidic than the common type, so when using it in recipes, you might need to adjust the quantity.

Historically, sorrel was extensively used by both the Egyptians and the Romans, to counteract the discomfort resulting from over indulgence in rich foods. This property is still associated with the culinary use of sorrel; it is often served as a sauce with fatty meats or oily fish, such as duck, pork, goose or salmon. It is also made into a sharp soup, to precede these rich foods. In Mediaeval times, sorrel was recommended for people suffering from fevers and inflammations. It was also prescribed as a means of sharpening appetites, and as an antidote to scurvy, because of its high vitamin C content.

High in oxalic acid, sorrel should never be taken in vast quantities. It should also never be cooked in iron pans: the sorrel turns a very nasty black colour. Stainless steel knives are also recommended when cutting it although, like basil, I would recommend simply tearing or shredding with your fingers. Because of its acidity, the juice extracted from leaves is commonly used in Lapland as a substitute for rennet, to curdle milk during the cheese-making process.

The classic way of preparing sorrel is to wash the leaves and strip off the green parts from the ribs; stack them up on a board and either snip them with scissors or shred them with your fingers. The usual way of cooking it is to make a purée by cooking for a couple of minutes in melted butter or, as in France, in lard or bacon fat. Some recipes for sorrel soup advise cooking it before blending all the ingredients together. This way, however, the soup can very quickly turn a rusty brown colour: for a truer, fresh, bright green colour and bolder taste, add the sorrel at the last minute – when you are blending the soup. Try sorrel as a filling for omelettes or soufflés, or stirred into dishes made from lentils or beans. Add a few leaves towards the end of cooking a venison casserole, or a hearty fish stew (it is especially good with eel). For the freshest flavour, shred a few leaves into a salad, either to accompany rich fare, or as a starter, preceding a heavy main course. Sharp and refreshing, it makes a perfect appetiser.

Sorrel and Pine Kernel Soup

Some sorrel soups are very sharp indeed. The refreshing lemony taste of a sorrel soup is, I think, best suited to summer especially before a rather rich main course, as it sharpens the appetite. The addition of pine kernels adds a good contrasting buttery edge, for all nuts have a high fat content. This balances out the tartness of the sorrel. The soup is cooked very quickly to retain the wonderfully fresh flavour of both the sorrel and the spinach and also the bright colour. Most of the sorrel is cooked for a few minutes, then more is added towards the end, for extra colour and taste. If you like, this can be garnished with a few toasted pine kernels, just before serving, or, for added richness, top with a swirl of cream. (serves 4–5)

2 oz/50 g butter	5 oz/150 g sorrel, washed
3 oz/75 g pine kernels	salt, pepper
1 onion, peeled and finely chopped	
1 oz/25 g plain flour	To serve
1½ pints/900 ml hot chicken stock	cream (optional)
4 oz/125 g young spinach, washed	toasted pine kernels (optional)

1. In a large saucepan, heat the butter, then fry the pine kernels gently, for about 3 minutes, until golden. Stir well, as they tend to burn quickly. Remove with a slotted spoon.

2. Add the onion and cook for about 3 minutes, until softened. Then add the flour and cook for about 2 minutes, stirring constantly. Pour in the hot chicken stock, then increase the heat and, stirring all the time, bring to the boil. Once it has come fully to the boil, add all the spinach and 4 oz/125 g of the sorrel. Stir well and cook for about 3 minutes, uncovered, over a fairly high heat.

3. Tip everything into a liquidiser (you may need to do this in 2 batches). Add the pine kernels and the remaining sorrel, and blend it all together. Season to taste and blend until smooth.

7. Reheat very gently, if necessary, and taste again for seasoning. Serve with a swirl of cream and some toasted pine kernels.

NOTE: The soup can be frozen. It still tastes good, but it loses some of its bright, fresh colour.

Chilled Sorrel Soup with Avocado

This is a delightfully appetising summer soup. I like to serve it in a large soup tureen, to be handed round the table, for it is decidedly moreish. The flavours are intriguing; it is rather spicy, from the cumin and coriander, and also fairly sharp, from the sorrel. The colour gives a clue about the ingredients, as it is delicate pale green – both from the sorrel and from the avocado. The low-fat natural yoghurt gives it a smooth, silky texture. It is the perfect dish to precede a rich or heavy main course, as it sharpens up the appetite. Accompany with warmed walnut or granary bread. (serves 3–4)

1 pint/600 ml light chicken stock	juice of 1 lime
¼ teaspoon ground coriander	¾ pint/450 ml low-fat unset
½ teaspoon ground cumin	natural yoghurt
3 oz/75 g sorrel, washed	3 spring onions, chopped
2 ripe avocados, peeled and sliced	salt, pepper

1. First, bring the chicken stock, coriander and cumin to the boil. Once it is bubbling, tear in the sorrel and cook for 1 minute, then remove from the heat and pour into a liquidiser. Purée, then push through a fine sieve and allow to cool, to room temperature.

2. Place the avocados, lime juice, yoghurt and spring onions into a food processor or blender. Process until smooth, then add the cooled stock. You may need to do this in batches, depending on the size of your processor. Blend everything together, then season to taste with salt and pepper. You might want to use a balloon whisk for a final blending by hand.

3. Place in the fridge for at least 3 hours, or up to 8 hours. Then serve in chilled bowls.

NOTE: Do not freeze.

Sorrel and Goat's Cheese Soufflé

There are bold, strident flavours in this soufflé, depending on the type of cheese you use. Some goat's cheeses are fairly mild, when they are sold fresh and young, and although they have a distinctive taste, they do not have enough 'punch' to come through in a cooked dish, such as this soufflé. I would not, however, recommend one of the very mature cheeses, which are incredibly strong and decidedly 'goaty' in flavour. These would dominate the taste of the sorrel too much. Look out for a goat's cheese which has formed a soft rind (not a hard crusty one) and which is not too fresh, but not too old or mature. If there is a rind, be sure to remove it before incorporating into the sauce. The easiest way to remove the rind of soft cheeses is, first of all, to chill the cheese in the fridge, then dip a sharp knife into hot water, before cutting the rind. As with all soufflés, this must be served at once, so be sure your guests are already seated. Try not to open the oven door while it is cooking, or your gloriously risen soufflé will turn into a sunken, deflated soufflé: still very tasty, but not quite so spectacular to look at! (serves 4)

2 oz/50 g butter	4 oz/125 g goat's cheese, rind
1½ oz/40 g plain flour	removed, cubed
½ pint/300 ml milk	½ oz/15 g butter
3 eggs, separated, plus 1 egg white	4 oz/125 g sorrel
	salt, pepper

1. Preheat the oven to Gas 5/190°C/375°F. Heat the butter in a saucepan and then add the flour. Stir well, to form a roux, and cook for a couple of minutes, stirring all the time.

2. Gradually add the milk and whisk over a low heat until it thickens. Cook for about 3 minutes, then remove from the heat.

3. Add the egg yolks, beating well, then the goat's cheese and stir to combine.

4. Melt the butter in a saucepan and cook the sorrel for about 1 minute, until it just begins to wilt. Remove to a board and chop roughly, then add to the sauce.

5. Whisk the 4 egg whites until they form soft peaks, then gently fold a quarter of these into the sauce. Once this has been done, fold in the remaining egg whites very gently, using a cutting and folding action.

6. Butter a 2 pint/1.2 litre soufflé dish and pour in the mixture. Do not worry if you think it is rather a lot of mixture, it will rise beautifully. Bake in the centre of the preheated oven for about 30–35 minutes, until it is well-risen and golden brown. Only check inside the oven after 30 minutes, never before. Serve immediately.

NOTE: Do not freeze.

Sorrel and Anchovy Tart

This tart, rather like the Sorrel soup with avocado (see page 144), has intriguing flavours in it. First, there is beautifully short, buttery cheese pastry (which is, in fact, a good pastry for any savoury tart), then a filling of sorrel, which is tangy and sharp, mixed with cream and Mascarpone, and flavoured lightly with garlic and spring onions. The anchovies on top add a salty, savoury edge. It can be cut into tiny wedges and served with drinks before dinner or served as a starter. As a starter, I would suggest serving it with some fresh salad, perhaps of orange and chicory or cos lettuce and thin lemon slivers. You could also offer some creamy mayonnaise, flavoured with a couple of mashed anchovy fillets, or with dijon mustard. A slice of this tart, served warm, with a dollop of home-made mayonnaise, is truly delicious. (serves 6)

Pastry	Filling
7 oz/200 g plain flour, sifted	1 oz/25 g butter
2 oz/50 g freshly grated Parmesan cheese	2 garlic cloves, and finely chopped
½ teaspoon salt	4 spring onions, finely chopped
5 oz/150 g unsalted butter, diced	5 oz/150 g sorrel, shredded
1 egg	4 oz/125 g mascarpone cream cheese
1 tablespoon olive oil	¼ pint/150 ml double cream
	1 oz/25 g freshly grated Parmesan cheese
	3 eggs
	salt, pepper
	5–6 anchovy fillets

1. For the pastry, place the flour, cheese and salt in a food processor with the butter and process until it resembles breadcrumbs. Mix the egg with the oil and add to the pastry mixture. Process briefly, then bring together with your hand and chill in clingfilm for at least 1 hour.

2. Roll the pastry out as thinly as possible, without it breaking, to fit a 9 in/23 cm loose-bottom tart tin. You will have quite a lot of pastry left (it is not worth making less in the food processor). Either make some tiny tartlets in small pastry tins or pop the remaining pastry into the freezer for another day. Prick the pastry in the tin all over, then place in the fridge for several hours, preferably overnight, or for 30 minutes in the freezer.

3. Preheat the oven to Gas Mark 6/200°C/400°F. Line with foil and baking beans and bake blind in the preheated oven for 10 minutes. Remove the foil and bake for a further 5 minutes or until it is just cooked. Lower the heat to Gas Mark 5/190°C/375°F.

4. Allow the tart to cool slightly, while you make the filling.

5. Melt the butter in a saucepan and cook the garlic and spring onions for about 3 minutes, then add the shredded sorrel. Cook for only about 1–2 minutes, until the sorrel has just begun to wilt, then remove from the heat.

6. Beat together the Mascarpone, cream, Parmesan, eggs and salt and pepper, then stir in the sorrel mixture.

7. Carefully ladle this in to the tart. Top with the anchovies, arranging like spokes of a wheel, then bake in the oven for about 30 minutes, or until it is puffed up and golden brown.

8. Allow to cool to barely warm, then cut into wedges.

NOTE: This freezes well.

Warm Sorrel and Bacon Salad

Warm salads are fairly new and rather fashionable. They are, however, not one of those food trends which is meaningless. They are superb for various reasons. Firstly, you can incorporate ingredients into a salad which do not taste so good cold – for example chicken livers, bacon, black pudding. Secondly, they are good to eat during winter and autumn, rather than simply throughout the long, hot summer. The dressing is made in the frying pan; first fry the hot ingredients, then at the very end, add the vinegar, and allow it to sizzle before pouring over the salad leaves. The combination of sorrel, spinach and smoky bacon work very well indeed. Serve with fresh, warm rye or wholemeal bread to dunk into the tasty juices. (serves 3–4)

3 oz/75 g young sorrel, washed	3 tablespoons olive oil
4 oz/125 g young spinach, washed	4 oz/125 g smoked streaky bacon,
1 tablespoon hazlenut oil	cubed
salt, pepper	1 tablespoon raspberry vinegar

1. Remove the ribs from the sorrel and roughly tear the leaves into a salad bowl. Add the spinach, then gently toss these in the hazelnut oil, with some salt and pepper.

2. In a frying pan, heat the olive oil, then fry the bacon for about 8–10 minutes until it is crispy and golden. Once it is ready, pour in the vinegar, and stir well (beware: it will splatter!).

3. Pour the entire contents of the pan over the salad leaves. Toss very well. Serve at once.
   NOTE: Do not freeze.

Spicy Lentils with Sorrel

This is a variation on that famous Indian dish, dhal, which is usually made from lentils and various spices. My version is not very hot but subtly spicy, with the flavours of ginger, turmeric and cumin. Sorrel is then added to the dhal, just before serving. The result is a sharp, contrasting taste to complement the spicy lentils. Serve this either as a side dish to accompany Indian meat or fish dishes, or as a vegetarian course on its own. If you do not serve the lentils at once, you might need to stir in another tablespoon of olive oil just before serving, once you have reheated. If you have to reheat, do it over a very low heat, otherwise it might stick to the bottom of the pan and burn. (serves 4)

8 oz/250 g red lentils, rinsed	½ teaspoon ground cumin
¾ pint/450 ml water	salt, pepper
3 tablespoons groundnut oil	4 oz/125 g sorrel, washed, and
½ teaspoon ground ginger	shredded
½ teaspoon ground turmeric	1 tablespoon olive oil

1. First cook the lentils. Place them in a large saucepan with the water and bring to the boil. Boil rapidly for 10 minutes, then reduce to a simmer and cook for a further 20 minutes.

2. Heat 1 tablespoon of the groundnut oil and fry the three spices for half a minute, stirring well. Then tip these, with the oil, into the lentils. Season them well with salt and pepper.

3. In the same saucepan, heat the remaining 2 tablespoons groundnut oil, then drop in the shredded sorrel and cook for about 1–2 minutes, until just wilted.

4. Stir the sorrel with the oil into the lentils and season again to taste. Stir in the olive oil, then serve at once. NOTE: Do not freeze.

Salmon with Sorrel Sauce

This is a classic. In France, sorrel is used with salmon, in a creamy sauce, such as this one, and also as a stuffing for whole fish such as large trout. The sharp flavour permeates the juices to accompany the fish. In this recipe, it is essential to allow the liquid to reduce sufficiently. You must also cook the cream, when it is added, for a good 4–5 minutes to allow it to thicken. Many sorrel sauces have rather a lot of butter beaten in at the end, but I prefer adding only a little, really to give the finished sauce a glossy sheen. Serve this dish with buttered new potatoes and steamed green vegetables. (serves 4)

Sauce	½ oz/15 g butter
½ pint/300 ml fish stock	salt, pepper
¼ pint/150 ml dry white wine
3 shallots, peeled and chopped	Fish
¼ pint/150 ml double cream	4 medium-sized salmon steaks or fillets
3 oz/75 g sorrel leaves	1 tablespoon olive oil

1. For the sauce, bring the stock, wine and shallots to the boil, then lower the heat slightly and cook over a medium heat, until reduced to about one-third. (This could take up to as long as 10–15 minutes, depending on your saucepan.)
2. Meanwhile, cook the fish. Place the salmon on an oiled grill-tray and rub in the olive oil. Cook under a preheated grill for about 3–4 minutes each side, depending on the thickness.
3. Once the sauce has reduced, add the cream and cook until it has a sauce-like consistency. Then strain into a clean pan and bring slowly back to a simmer. Remove the central ribs from the sorrel and tear the leaves into the sauce. Cook for a maximum of 2 minutes, then remove from the heat. Season to taste with salt and pepper and whisk in the butter.
4. Pour the sauce around the salmon and serve at once. NOTE: Do not freeze.

Lamb Chops with Sorrel and Apple Relish

A tangy relish is served with plain grilled lamb chops, in this unusual but very simple recipe; it can also be served with pork chops. It is a last-minute dish, as, although you can prepare the ingredients for the relish in advance (keep them covered, in separate bowls), it is better not to combine them together until shortly before eating. The overall flavour of the relish is tangy and refreshing, which is ideal with a fatty meat such as lamb. (serves 4)

4 lamb chops	2 Granny Smith apples, unpeeled
1 tablespoon white wine vinegar	2 tomatoes, diced
salt, pepper	2 tablespoons capers
1 teaspoon sugar	4 oz/125 g sorrel, washed and shredded
1 teaspoon horseradish relish	1 tablespoon walnut oil

1. Grill the lamb chops for about 3–4 minutes each side, depending on how thick they are.
2. Meanwhile, make the relish: combine the vinegar, salt, pepper, sugar and horseradish relish in a bowl. Then, without peeling them, grate in the apples, add the tomatoes, capers and finally the sorrel. Mix everything together well, then stir in the walnut oil and check once more for seasoning. Serve at room temperature with the lamb. NOTE: Do not freeze.

chapter 18

sweet cicely

The mention of the herb sweet cicely always evokes the same response: what a wonderfully old-fashioned sounding name and it is, indeed, an old-fashioned herb, used extensively in the past. It is a stout, umbelliferous plant, growing between 2 and 5 feet tall, with fern-like, lacy leaves and white flowers which appear early in the year. A perennial, grown from seed or propagated by root division, it is a shade-loving plant, and is sufficiently decorative to be used in an ornamental border. An indication of the flavour of the leaves lies in its Latin name, *Myrrhis odorata,* which, in turn, was derived from the Greek word for myrrh. It is fragrant and has a sweet anise taste, reminiscent of liquorice.

If more people recognised it in the wild, perhaps it would be used more in the kitchen, for it grows wild in woods, hedges and along roadsides all over northern Europe. It is particularly common, however, in northern England and southern Scotland. In the past, every possible part of the plant was used. The thick roots were boiled or shredded and added to salads; the green seeds were also added to vegetables or salads, or used as a spicy flavouring. In Germany sweet cicely is still often used, particularly in conjunction with tarragon, in many recipes. In France it is sometimes served as an appetiser: the leaves are first dipped in batter, then deep-fried and served hot and crispy. Although I cannot wholeheartedly recommend the use of boiled sweet cicely roots, I would urge you to try the leaves in your cooking, for they are both versatile and useful.

The leaves are excellent in all sorts of salads, for their texture is soft and their flavour delicate. Because of its anise flavour, it goes well with all sorts of seafood and certain vegetables: cabbage, broccoli or spinach, for example. But it is with sharp tart fruits, such as gooseberries, rhubarb or currants, that it is not only a good old-fashioned flavouring, but also (essential to these diet-obsessed days) a 'sugar-saver'. It merits this title, because its natural sweetness means you need to add less sugar when cooking fruit. Make a rhubarb crumble or gooseberry fool and use only half the normal amount of sugar when you mix in some sweet cicely, or add it to fresh fruit salads, fruit compotes, or summer fruit ice-creams. In these health-conscious days, how refreshing to find a natural way of avoiding unnecessary calories!

Outside the kitchen, sweet cicely seeds have been used by proud housekeepers to polish oak furniture and floors. When the wood became dry, the seeds were rubbed into the surface, in a soft cloth. The result was a high polish and a very pleasant, aromatic scent.

Modern herbalists recommend sweet cicely as an aid to strengthen the digestion. It is also prescribed for bladder disorders, flatulence and coughs.

I should like to see more fuss being made of this lovely, underrated herb. It is believed to be a pick-me-up, meant to 'cheer the spirits', so why bother with anti-depressants, when you can have sweet cicely instead!

Herb Salad with Flowers

Summer is the time for this colourful and interesting salad. Depending on what you have in your garden, you can go mad! But at first, ensure the flowers you want to use are edible. I suggest nasturtiums, heartsease pansies, calendula (pot marigold) or any of the herb flowers. However, since you want the preponderant flavour to be sweet cicely, try to restrict your herb flowers to a very small handful. To prepare the petals, simply give them a good shake, upside down, to allow any 'wildlife' to be dislodged. Only wash and shake dry if absolutely necessary. For the salad leaves, I prefer to use softer textured ones, such as rocket, young spinach or lamb's lettuce, rather than crunchy cos or iceberg. It is particularly important to toss this salad at the very last minute, as flower petals are rather delicate and will spoil if left in the oily dressing for too long.

1 tablespoon fresh herbs such as chervil, dill, bronze fennel, parsley, roughly chopped	<u>Dressing</u>
	1 tablespoon raspberry vinegar
	2 tablespoons sunflower oil
2 tablespoons sweet cicely, roughly chopped	2 tablespoons extra-virgin olive oil
	salt, pepper
1 salad bowlful of prepared salad leaves, torn	
edible flowers	

1. Using your hands, mix the herbs and sweet cicely into the salad leaves. Then mix in about half of the flowers, separating the petals from the larger flowers.

2. Mix all the dressing ingredients and toss over the salad at the last minute. Garnish with the remaining flowers and serve at once. NOTE: Do not freeze.

Sweet Cicely Soda Bread

Soda bread is a very easy bread to make. While I was learning to make it, I kept reminding myself that the principle is very similar to scone-making. What is required, in other words, is a light touch, not the table-bashing bread-maker's touch! You can use all sorts of different ingredients in this bread, but usually there is a mixture of wholemeal and plain flour, with either buttermilk or sour milk (which incidentally make the best scones). I have added some oats for an even rougher texture. The sweet cicely gives it a good colour, but, more important, a wonderfully subtle aniseed flavour. This particular taste, I find, is good to accompany any fish dish, from lobster thermidor to fried fish. Otherwise serve it with a bowl of piping hot fish or vegetable soup. It is best eaten on the day it is made; next day, cut it into thick slices and toast under the grill. (makes 1 loaf)

8 oz/250 g plain flour, sifted	1 teaspoon salt
4 oz/125 g wholemeal flour	2 oz/50 g butter, diced
2 oz/50 g porridge oats (not jumbo oat flakes)	2 tablespoons sweet cicely, finely chopped
1 teaspoon bicarbonate of soda	8–9 fl oz/250–275 ml buttermilk
1 teaspoon cream of tartar	or sour milk

1. Preheat the oven to Gas Mark 7/220°C/425°F and butter a baking tray. Combine the flours, oats, bicarbonate of soda and cream of tartar in a bowl. Add the salt. Rub in the butter, until it resembles breadcrumbs. Stir in the sweet cicely. Pour in just enough buttermilk or sour

milk to form a soft but not too sticky dough. Combine, then turn on to a lightly floured board and very gently knead as if you were making scones, for 2 minutes.

3. Shape into a round, flatten out a little, then, using a sharp knife, mark out a cross in the surface. Place on the buttered baking tray. Bake for about 25–30 minutes until cooked.

5. Remove to a wire rack, cover lightly with a clean cloth and allow to cool. Serve it barely warm. NOTE: The bread freezes very well.

Eyemouth Tart

I first tasted Eyemouth Tart at a Borders food fair. Mrs Burke, the baker, who specialises in home-baking in the Borders of Scotland, kindly offered to provide me with the recipe. Mine is similar to hers, but with a little bit of this and that added! I was very keen indeed on the tart as it reminded me of a childhood favourite, Border Tart, which was one of my mother's regulars. The difference in the Eyemouth Tart is the addition of coconut, walnuts and cherries. I have added sweet cicely to the pastry. This gives not only a good flavour, but also a lovely variegated appearance to the finished tart. Although I had never used sweet cicely with dried fruit and nuts, as opposed to fresh fruit, I think it works very well indeed. Serve the tart barely warm or at room temperature, with a cup of afternoon tea, or as a pudding with clotted cream. (serves 6)

<u>Pastry</u>
2 tablespoons sweet cicely, chopped
5 oz/150 g plain flour, sifted
a pinch of salt
2 oz/50 g caster sugar
2 oz/50 g ground almonds
3 oz/75 g unsalted butter, cubed
1 egg

<u>Icing</u>
4 oz/125 g icing sugar, sifted
1–2 tablespoons lemon juice
1 teaspoon sunflower oil

<u>Filling</u>
2 oz/50 g walnuts, roughly chopped
2 oz/50 g currants
2 oz/50 g raisins
2 oz/50 g desiccated coconut
2 oz/50 g glacé cherries, chopped
   (I prefer the undyed ones)
3 oz/75 g soft dark brown sugar
2 oz/50 g butter, melted
1 egg, beaten

1. For the pastry, mix the first 5 ingredients in a food processor, then add the butter and process briefly. Slowly add the egg and process until it forms a ball. Wrap in clingfilm and refrigerate for at least 2 hours (or in place in the freezer for 15 minutes).

2. Then roll out to fit a shallow, loose-bottom 9 in/23 cm pie tin. Prick all over, then either refrigerate overnight, or place in the freezer for 30 minutes.

3. Preheat the oven to Gas Mark 5/190°C/375°F. Bake the tart case blind, with foil and baking beans, in a preheated oven for 10 minutes, then remove the foil and beans and continue to bake for a further 5–8 minutes, until just cooked. Remove the tart case and lower the oven temperature to Gas Mark 4/180°C/350°F.

4. Mix the first 5 filling ingredients, then beat the sugar and butter together and mix into the fruit and nuts. Add the egg and stir well to combine. Pour this into the tart case and bake in the oven for about 30–35 minutes, until it is just set and golden.

5. For the icing, mix the icing sugar with sufficient lemon juice to form a thick glacé icing, then add the oil (this ensures that it does not become too hard). Carefully spread this over the cooled tart and allow to set. Serve the tart in slices. NOTE: This can be frozen.

Scallops with Cabbage and Sweet Cicely

I absolutely adore scallops, which should be succulent, moist and firm, never flabby or watery. For dishes such as this where they are simply seared, it is essential that the scallops are not frozen. It is also essential that the pan is very hot indeed when you put them in. Be brave and allow it to heat up for quite some time. The pan should, of course, be very heavy-based; otherwise, the scallops will burn. Sweet cicely goes well with both the cabbage and the scallops; the aniseed flavour suits both vegetable and shellfish perfectly. This is a last-minute dish, so have everything ready in advance and simply cook at the very last minute. As a main course, serve this with a green salad and hot bread or sauté potatoes, but I also think it makes a good starter, if followed by a meaty or vegetable-based main course. (serves 4)

12 plump fresh scallops (dark threads removed and scallops cleaned)	12 oz/375 g white cabbage, sliced
1 tablespoon olive oil	juice of 1 lime
salt, pepper	7 fl oz/200 ml crème fraîche
1 oz/25 g butter	2 tablespoons sweet cicely, finely chopped

1. Toss the prepared scallops in a dish with the olive oil. Season with salt and pepper. Cover with clingfilm and leave for about 30 minutes.
2. Melt the butter, then add the cabbage and lime juice. Over a medium heat, cook the cabbage, uncovered, stirring for about 5 minutes.
3. Then increase the heat and add the crème fraîche and sweet cicely. Cook for a further 2–3 minutes, then taste and season.
4. Meanwhile, heat a heavy-based frying pan to very hot indeed. Add the scallops, which are already coated in oil so no further cooking fat is required. Cook for about 3 minutes altogether, depending on how thick they are. Turn after 1 minute.
5. To serve, place a spoonful of the creamy cabbage on to warm plates, then top with the scallops. Serve at once. NOTE: Do not freeze.

Red Fruit Salad

The flavours of these fruits are enhanced greatly by a little sweet cicely. You can use any red fruits, but I do recommend the combination of strawberries, plums and black grapes. Raspberries or tayberries are also good substitutes. Serve this after a rich or creamy main course, as it is light, refreshing and summery. Offer thick cream or Greek yoghurt alongside. (serves 4–6)

1 lb/500 g strawberries, hulled, sliced
¾ lb/375 g of plums and black grapes, cut into slices
1 tablespoon caster sugar
2 tablespoons orange juice
1 tablespoon sweet cicely, finely chopped

1. Place the fruit in a large bowl, then spoon over the sugar and orange juice. Toss well to mix. Leave for at least 30 minutes.
2. Just before serving, toss in the sweet cicely and gently mix together. Serve at room temperature, not from the fridge. NOTE: Do not freeze.

Rhubarb Crumble Cake

Rhubarb crumble is often given a bad press, especially if memories are fired by school dinner crumbles, served with garish, lumpy custard. But a well-made crumble is a wonderful, old-fashioned pudding, which is more versatile than it sounds. You can mix oats into the crumble, or use dark, soft sugar to make it fudgy; or demerara sugar to make it crunchy. This recipe is a cake mixture, topped with rhubarb mixed with its ideal mate, sweet cicely, then topped with an oaty crumble mixture. The cake is delicious served either warm or cold, as a pudding with thick cream or with a morning cup of dark roast coffee. Remember to drain the rhubarb very well after it has been cooked, otherwise your cake will be soggy. (serves 4–6)

<u>Cake</u>
8 oz/250 g plain flour
2 teaspoons baking powder
a pinch of salt
2 oz/50 g butter, softened
4 oz/125 g caster sugar
1 large egg
4 fl oz/125 ml milk

<u>Filling</u>
1 lb/500 g rhubarb, washed and chopped
2 oz/50 g sugar
2 tablespoons sweet cicely, finely chopped
<u>Topping</u>
1 oz/25 g plain flour
1 oz/25 g oats (either porridge oats or oat flakes)
2 oz/50 g demerara sugar
2 oz/50 g butter, cubed

1. For the cake, sift the flour, baking powder and salt into a bowl. Cream the butter and sugar together until soft, then beat in the egg and milk. Add the flour in batches and combine until well mixed. Spoon into a buttered 7 in/18 cm loose-bottomed cake tin. Preheat the oven to Gas Mark 5/190°C/375°F.

2. Mix the rhubarb and sugar in a saucepan, then cook for 5–10 minutes, until just cooked. Drain very well over a sieve, then stir in the sweet cicely. Spoon this over the cake mix.

3. For the topping, mix the flour, oats and sugar together. Rub in the butter and sprinkle the crumble over the rhubarb.

4. Bake in the preheated oven for about 40–45 minutes, until well-risen. Test with a cocktail stick: it should come out clean when pushed into the centre.

NOTE: This freezes well.

Redcurrant and Apple Lattice Pie

Lattice pies and tarts always look so good and yet they are very easy to make. There is, in fact, a special device whereby you can roll out the pastry and cut it into a very neat lattice work top. But I find that unless the pastry is rather hard, it tends to crumble or break up. For good short, crumbly pastry, it is easier to cut by hand. Use either a sharp knife or a pastry cutter with serrated edges and cut out 8–10 strips of pastry. Then, starting at one end of the pie, place one in position across the pie. Set the next strip over the first at a right angle to it. Then return to the first side and position the third strip. Continue by alternating the side you start from and gradually you will have a very acceptable lattice. This pie is made in a deep pie tin, so it is bulging with the fruit. The sweet cicely in the fruit mixture means you need less sugar than normal. Serve this warm, with either Greek yoghurt or lightly whipped cream. (serves 6–8)

Pastry
9 oz/275 g plain flour
5 oz/150 g butter, cubed
3 oz/75 g icing sugar
a pinch of salt
zest of 1 lemon
1 large egg (size 1)

To finish the pastry
1 small egg yolk
1 heaped tablespoon semolina
milk and caster sugar, to glaze

Filling
1½ lb/750 g cooking apples
    (such as Bramleys), peeled,
    cored and chopped into dice
1 lb/500 g redcurrants
5 oz/150 g caster sugar
2 tablespoons sweet cicely, finely
    chopped

1. For the pastry, place the first 5 ingredients in a food processor and process until the mixture resembles breadcrumbs. Add the egg and process briefly, then make into a ball, wrap in clingfilm and refrigerate for about 2 hours.

2. Then roll out three-quarters of the pastry, to fit a buttered 9½ in/24 cm deep, loose-bottomed tin. Prick all over, then brush all over the base and sides with the small egg yolk. Put in the refrigerator for 1 hour. Roll out the remaining pastry and, using a pastry cutter, cut out 8–10 lattice strips. Place these on a floured board and chill with the pie case for 1 hour.

3. After the hour, remove and sprinkle the semolina over the base of the pie. Preheat the oven to Gas Mark 4/180°C/350°F.

4. For the filling, mix together the apples, redcurrants, sugar and sweet cicely and then pile the filling into the pie case. Carefully place the lattice strips on top, one side after another, to form an overlapping lattice. Then brush the top with milk and sprinkle over a little caster sugar. (I like to use a sugar sprinkler for this.)

5. Bake in the preheated oven for 50–60 minutes, until the pastry is golden brown. Cool for about 15 minutes, then decant carefully.

NOTE: This pie freezes well. I prefer to freeze it in its tin, for easy reheating.

Gooseberry and Sweet Cicely Cheesecake

Cheesecakes have been in and out of fashion. In the 1970s and 1980s you could not go to any party without being served some form of cheesecake, often decorated with segments of mandarin oranges or chocolate flakes. At their best, they were home-made gelatine-set ones or baked ones; at their worst, they were mixed up from dubious-quality packets. Then, suddenly, they were no longer de rigueur. Flying in the face of fashion, however, I proudly present my favourite cheesecake: I have always loved the baked types, as I enjoyed many baked cheesecakes in Finland, always packed full of berries – lingonberries, blueberries, cranberries or even the most exquisite cloudberries. The flavour of sweet cicely goes beautifully with sharp, tart fruits, so it is the perfect partner for gooseberries in this creamy, old-fashioned cheesecake. (serves 8)

Base
6 oz/175 g gingernut biscuits
6 oz/175 g digestive biscuits
4 oz/125 g melted butter

Filling
13 oz/400 g cream cheese
2 eggs
the juice of 1 lemon
5 oz/150 g caster sugar
12 oz/375 g gooseberries, topped and tailed
1 heaped tablespoon sweet cicely, chopped

Topping
½ pint/300 ml sour cream
2 oz/50 g caster sugar

1. For the base, process the biscuits into crumbs, then mix with the melted butter. Press into a deep, lightly buttered, 9½ in/24 cm loose-bottomed tin and chill.

2. Preheat the oven to Gas Mark 4/180°C/350°F. For the filling, beat the cream cheese, eggs, lemon juice and 3 oz/75 g sugar together (I use a whisk), until smooth, then pour into the base. Bake in the middle of the preheated oven for 30 minutes, then remove.

3. Meanwhile, cook the gooseberries with the remaining 2 oz/50 g sugar for about 10 minutes, until soft. Drain well, over a sieve. Then, using a potato masher, mash together with the sweet cicely.

4. Once the cheesecake has been removed from the oven, allow it to cool for 5 minutes, then carefully spread the gooseberry mixture over the top.

5. For the topping, beat the sour cream with 2 oz/50 g sugar and slowly pour over the gooseberries. Return to the oven and bake for a further 15–20 minutes, until just set. Turn off the heat and keep the cheesecake in the turned-off oven for at least an hour, preferably overnight. (This means the surface will be smooth, not sunken.)

6. Serve at room temperature, in slices.

NOTE: This freezes very well.

chapter 19

tarragon

The tarragon we are most familiar with is often referred to as French tarragon. Its botanical name is *Artemisia dracunculis*. Dracunculis is Latin for 'little dragon', as it was reputedly used to cure bites and stings from venomous creatures including, presumably, serpents and snakes. Russian tarragon (*Artemisia dracunculoides*) has a very inferior flavour, paler leaves and a discernibly different taste. It certainly does not have the delicate yet highly perfumed flavour which we associate with French tarragon. French tarragon is a native of southern Europe and parts of Asia, whereas Russian tarragon is a Siberian wild plant.

The plant, which can grow to about 3 feet tall, is a bushy perennial, which fares best in well-drained soil and a sheltered, preferably sunny, location. It should always have protection from harsh northerly and easterly winds, but it is a fairly hardy plant; add it to your herb garden stalwarts or, for a winter supply, keep a pot of tarragon on a sunny window-ledge. Its leaves are shiny, long and narrow and fine enough for chopping into even the most refined of sauces. I find the best way to remove the leaves is to pluck them gently from the stem, not to use scissors. As with most herbs, pick at the last possible moment to keep its fresh taste and beautiful bright green colour.

Nowadays tarragon is appreciated most for its use in the kitchen but in the past it was believed to have remedial properties. Infusions, or 'tisanes', were said to aid digestive problems such as flatulence or heartburn; and its roots were frequently used as a cure for painful toothache. It was also once considered to be an aphrodisiac, but then, which plant was not?

Tarragon enhances many chicken and fish dishes. Tarragon Chicken is a recipe which most cooks will have in their repertoire: chicken is poached or roasted, then coated with a creamy sauce made from the chicken stock, double cream and fresh sprigs of tarragon. It is also excellent in egg dishes and with vegetables such as artichokes, mushrooms and marrow. Its warm flavour makes it a perfect contrast to cool summer vegetables and all sorts of salad leaves. It has a natural affinity with butter: a round of tarragon-flavoured butter atop a piece of roast poultry or fried steak is simple and very effective. Light butter sauces are also enhanced by fresh tarragon. Since its main use is in fairly delicate dishes – sole rather than tuna; chicken rather than wood pigeon – it should always be added with discretion, tasting as you add.

Dried tarragon is readily available but, like so many other dried herbs, it is only a little tastier than straw. It is best to quick-freeze tarragon leaves or convert them into vinegar for use when fresh tarragon is scarce. Tarragon vinegar (see page 162), is perhaps the best known way of preserving the herb and is quicker to make than many herb vinegars because of its rather pungent flavour. It only needs about 10 days of steeping; others, such as marjoram or basil, need up to 3 weeks. The vinegar is found in many of the well-known classics of French cuisine, for example béarnaise, ravigote or hollandaise sauces and many soups, creams and purées.

Courgette and Tarragon Tortilla

The Spanish tortilla, a type of vegetable omelette, is usually cooked in, and then served from, a frying pan. My tortilla is started off on the top of the stove, then finished off in the oven, so use a pan suitable for both. The combination of tarragon with eggs is classic; the herb is also excellent with any of the marrow family such as courgettes. When serving it warm, I like to top the tortilla with grated cheese before cooking. Cheddar is rather too strong for this, so I prefer another great English cheese, Cheshire, which is also an excellent cooking cheese. If you intend to eat the tortilla cold (you can invert the whole omelette on to foil to take on a picnic), then I think it is better without cheese, but try it both ways to decide for yourself. (serves 4–6)

> 1 large courgette (about 10 oz/300 g), wiped clean
> 3 tablespoons olive oil
> 1 medium onion, chopped
> 4 potatoes (about 1 lb/500 g) peeled, and cubed
> 2 tablespoons tarragon, freshly chopped
> 6 eggs, beaten
> 2 oz/50 g Cheshire cheese, grated

1. Preheat the oven to Gas Mark 4/180°C/350°F. Cut the unpeeled courgette into thin slices. Heat the oil in a 10 in/25 cm pan and fry the onion gently for about 3 minutes. Add the potatoes, and fry for a further 10–15 minutes, until they are just tender. Add the courgettes and fry for another 3 minutes, stirring well. Remove from the heat

2. Beat the tarragon with the eggs and plenty of salt (at least ¾ teaspoon) and pepper, then tip this all over the vegetables. Top with the grated cheese. Bake for about 30 minutes, until the eggs are just set.

3. Wait for at least 15 minutes before cutting into wedges, or leave until it is completely cold, then turn out on to foil, wrap and pack for your picnic. NOTE: Do not freeze.

Tarragon Vinegar

Tarragon vinegar is perhaps the best-known and most useful of all herb vinegars. It can be used in classic French sauces such as Béarnaise, and often in mayonnaise, vinaigrette or Hollandaise sauce. Many herbs can be used in exactly the same way, to make other types of herb vinegars. They are useful not only to dress your salad or add flavour to your sauces but, nicely labelled, they also make delightful gifts. The best herbs for vinegars, apart from tarragon, are basil, marjoram, thyme and mint. Do not be put off by the colour of the herbs as they are macerating in the vinegar – they will lose their bright fresh green colour almost immediately and turn a sludgy mud colour but it is the flavour, not the colour that is important. (makes 12 fl oz/ 350 ml)

> 12 fl oz/350 ml white wine vinegar
> approx 1 oz/25 g long sprigs of tarragon (about 6 sprigs)

1. Push the tarragon sprigs into the bottle of vinegar and screw on the lid tightly. Place on a windowsill (sunny, if possible) and leave for 10–14 days. Every time you pass, give the bottle a really good shake.

2. After the fortnight, strain the vinegar into a clean bottle, pop in a fresh sprig of tarragon and replace the lid. Keep in a dark place.

Marinated Feta Cheese

For this cheese recipe you must use Greek Feta, not the Danish variety, which has less flavour and the texture becomes rubbery when cooked or marinated. The Feta can be kept in its jar for up to 3 weeks, in a cool place. If you keep it in the fridge remove it an hour before using to allow the oil to melt. (It solidifies in the fridge.) Apart from serving the cheese drizzled with some of the accompanying oil in an antipasti platter, with black olives and a tomato salad, use in a classic Greek salad, or grill the cheese very quickly and splash with Ouzo just before serving, as a starter served with country bread. (serves 4–6)

8–10 oz/250–300 g Greek Feta cheese
4–5 short sprigs tarragon
7–10 fl oz/200–300 ml extra-virgin olive oil

1. Cut up the Feta into squares or rectangles, about ¾ in/2 cm thick. Place them in a Kilner jar with leaves of tarragon between each layer. Top up with sufficient olive oil to just cover. (The amount will depend on the width and depth of the jar.) Screw on the lid tightly. Marinate for at least 24 hours, keeping in a cool place (or in the fridge in summer time).

4. Serve as part of an antipasti platter. NOTE: Do not freeze.

Marinated Goat's Cheese with Spinach Salad

For this recipe, follow the marinated Feta procedure (see above) using either a log ('bûche') of goat's milk cheese or individual 'crottins'. I use an 8 oz/250 g log and cut it into 5 or 6 thick slices. If the cheese you use has developed a rind, try to remove it neatly, as it will impede the absorption of the oil and herb flavours. If, however, it begins to look messy (most of the cheese often comes away with the rind), then leave it, but prick the rind all over with a very fine skewer. As a change to grilling the cheese (or baking, in a fairly hot oven – Gas Mark 5/190°C/375°F for about for 8–10 minutes), use the cheese, cut up, in tarts or omelettes or tossed into pasta. (serves 4)

4 thick slices brown or granary bread
4 pieces of marinated goat's cheese (see above)
2 tablespoons olive oil from the jar of cheese
2 tablespoons walnut oil
1 tablespoon tarragon vinegar (or white wine vinegar)
salt, pepper
8–10 oz/250–300 g young spinach, washed

1. Set the grill to high. Using a pastry cutter, cut out 4 rounds of bread, the same diameter as the cheese. Place the bread on a grillproof tray and grill it on one side.

2. Place a round of cheese on the untoasted side of each, drizzle over a teaspoon or so of the oil from the jar, then grill for about 2–3 minutes until the cheese is just becoming golden. Watch it carefully; if you leave it too long, you will have a cheesy puddle.

3. Meanwhile, shake the remaining 1½ tablespoons of oil from the cheese marinade with the walnut oil, vinegar and salt and pepper together in a screw-top jar. Place the spinach in a large bowl and toss over the dressing. Arrange the leaves on to individual plates and top with a goat's cheese toast just before serving. NOTE: Do not freeze.

Mushroom and Tarragon Lasagne

Mushrooms and tarragon go extremely well together. In this recipe, they are mixed into a thick smooth sauce, layered with lasagne and topped with Parmesan cheese. Try to find interesting mushrooms – I like meaty-textured Paris browns or chestnut mushrooms for this dish, although flat cap or button mushrooms will do. Put in a few soaked, dried, wild mushrooms such as ceps (porcini) or girolles, if you have some in the larder. Add some of their soaking liquor to the sauce, for extra flavour. I also like to add the merest hint of truffle oil just before serving, after the lasagne is out of the oven. This is, however, purely personal; my husband hates this smelly addition, so try it for yourself and see. Only use best quality oil, and use no more than 2–3 drops, or the tarragon taste will be overpowered. As with all lasagne dishes, allow at least 10–15 minutes standing time before serving – apart from not burning your tongue, it cuts far more easily. It does not matter whether you use the pre-cooked or regular dry pasta, or fresh sheets of lasagne; simply follow packet instructions. I would, however, recommend that for the pre-cooked variety, you soak the sheets in hot water for at least 2 minutes, drain well, then assemble as normal. (serves 4)

6 sheets lasagne	1 pint/600 ml creamy milk
1 lb/500 g fresh mushrooms, cleaned	2 tablespoons tarragon, freshly
3 oz/75 g butter	chopped
1 tablespoon olive oil	salt, pepper
2½ oz/65 g plain flour	2 oz/50 g freshly grated Parmesan

1. If necessary, cook the lasagne (or soak) according to packet instructions.

2. Slice the mushrooms. Heat 2 oz/50 g of the butter in a pan, and gently fry the mushrooms for about 4–5 minutes, then remove with a slotted spoon.

3. Put the remaining 1 oz/25 g butter and the oil in to the pan, then add the flour and stir for about 1 minute. Gradually add the milk, whisking all the time, then simmer for about 5 minutes, until thick and smooth. Add the tarragon and the mushrooms and season to taste.

4. Preheat the oven to Gas Mark 4/180°C/350°F. Oil a lasagne dish (mine is 10 in/25 cm x 8 in/20 cm). Place 2 sheets of lasagne on the base, then a third of the mushroom sauce, then 2 more lasagne sheets, then more sauce, then the final lasagne sheets. Spoon over the remaining sauce and top with the Parmesan.

5. Bake in the preheated oven for 45–50 minutes, until golden brown. Leave to stand for at least 10 minutes before cutting. NOTE: Do not freeze.

Crab with Vodka and Pasta

This bizarre combination works really well together, but do try to look for fresh or frozen crabmeat. The quality of tinned crab is usually inferior. I like to use a mixture of white and brown meat – more white than brown, as the brown has a much stronger flavour. The vodka adds a certain punchiness to the sauce; if you do not have any, use whisky instead (only 1 tablespoon), but the flavour will be more discernible. Since vodka is rather a neutral-tasting spirit, it is ideal, for it adds that edge without imparting a particular flavour. Keep tasting towards the end of cooking, to see if you need more tarragon: depending on the ratio of white to brown crabmeat you use, you may need more. For the pasta, use either linguine, capellini or spaghetti. Do not top this pasta dish with Parmesan cheese. (serves 4)

1½ oz/40 g butter
2–3 shallots, peeled and chopped
12 oz/375 g crabmeat
   (8 oz/250 g white, 4 oz/125 g brown)
2 tablespoons vodka
¼ pint/150 ml double cream

3 tablespoons tarragon, freshly
   chopped
salt, pepper
12 oz/375 g linguine, capellini or
   spaghetti
extra-virgin olive oil, to finish

1. Melt the butter in a saucepan and gently fry the shallots for 2–3 minutes until golden. Add the crab and stir thoroughly.

2. Spoon in the vodka, increase the heat and bubble for 1 minute. Pour in the cream and lower the heat.

3. Add the tarragon, then simmer for 4–5 minutes. Taste and season.

4. Meanwhile, cook the pasta according to packet timings, then drain and toss with the crab sauce. Drizzle over some olive oil, just before serving.

NOTE: Do not freeze.

Parsnip and Chicken with Tarragon and Garlic

This is a variation on that classic, tarragon chicken, which can be very rich if it is laden with too much cream. In this recipe chicken thighs, which are very inexpensive, are tossed with whole garlic cloves, parsnips and tarragon in good olive oil, then roasted in a hot oven. The result is succulent chicken subtly flavoured with garlic and tarragon. The parsnips become crunchy outside and moist inside, as do the garlic cloves, which are eaten as you would a shallot or baby onion. By roasting the cloves whole, they taste sweeter than raw, chopped garlic. I like to serve this with warm crusty bread and a salad tossed in a light dressing of sunflower oil and lemon juice. (serves 6)

6 tablespoons olive oil
6 large garlic cloves, peeled and left whole
2 heaped tablespoons tarragon, freshly chopped
6 skinless chicken thighs,
3 large parsnips, peeled, cut into chunks and parboiled for 2 minutes
salt, pepper

1. Preheat the oven to Gas Mark 7/220°C/425°F. In a bowl, combine the oil with the garlic, tarragon, chicken and parsnips, turning them over to cool with the oil.

2. Pour everything into a roasting tin and season with salt and pepper. Roast in the preheated oven for 10 minutes, then reduce the heat to Gas Mark 5/190°C/375°F and continue roasting for a further 20–30 minutes, until the chicken is just cooked through. (Check by piercing with a sharp knife – if the juice is clear, it is done.)

4. Serve at once, with a little of the pan juices poured over.

NOTE: Do not freeze.

Stir-fried Chicken with Lemongrass and Tarragon

The flavours in this dish are clean-tasting, slightly hot and wonderfully aromatic. The combination of lemongrass, garlic, chilli and spring onion is a base for many Thai stir-fries. The addition of tarragon is unusual, since coriander or basil are more commonly used in Far Eastern cooking. The resulting flavour, although not authentically Thai, is however, pungent, delicate and delicious. I use a coffee grinder (well-washed after the Kenyan beans!) to make the paste for the stir-fry. Depending on the size of your food processor, you could use that instead, remembering that some machines do not work well with small amounts. Or, if you prefer, use a mortar and pestle. I have added sugar-snap peas for crunch and colour, but you could substitute green beans or mange-touts. (serves 4)

2 thick spring onion, chopped
2 fat stalks lemongrass, coarse outer layers removed, chopped
2 garlic cloves, peeled and chopped
½ fresh green chilli, deseeded and roughly chopped
4 tablespoons fresh tarragon
juice of ½ lime
4 small boneless skinned chicken breasts
salt, pepper
2 tablespoons sunflower oil
4 oz/125 g sugar-snap peas
fresh tarragon, to garnish (optional)

1. For the paste, place the first 5 ingredients in the grinder, then add the lime juice. Process until the paste is well combined. (At this stage it can be kept in the fridge for a day.)

2. Cut the chicken into small strips and season with salt and pepper. Heat the oil in a large frying pan or wok until very hot. Add the paste and fry for 1 minute, stirring constantly. Add the chicken and stir-fry for 2 minutes, then add the peas and cook for a further 3–5 minutes, until the chicken is just cooked.

3. Serve at once garnished with fresh tarragon, if desired.

NOTE: Do not freeze.

chapter 20

thyme

I shall always remember my first encounter with thyme. It arouses vivid memories, not of its taste, but of its powerful smell. It was in the dry, sunny hills of Provence and we stopped the car for a break. My French friend leapt out to pick huge bunches of aromatic wild thyme. It is a bushy plant with woody stems, small grey-green leaves and pinkish-purple flowers. At home, it was put into all sorts of tomato sauces and vegetable dishes such as ratatouille, stuffed aubergine or onions; it was cooked with grilled lamb or rabbit casserole. I also tasted some local honey which was scented with thyme. This variety of wild thyme (*Thymus serpyllum*) is found all over Mediterranean lands (where it is at its most aromatic) and is now established all over North America and in Britain, where it grows on heathland, hills and dunes.

However, it is garden thyme (*Thymus vulgaris*) which we are most likely to use here. This came originally from southern Europe, and is now to be found in many varieties, for example English 'broad-leaved' and French 'narrow-leaved'. It grows easily from seed or from rooted cuttings and prefers a light, well-drained soil. It is a popular rockery plant, not only for its looks, but also for its pleasant fragrance. The tiny thyme flowers are similar in taste to the leaves – highly aromatic, warming and earthy. The easiest way to remove both the leaves and the flowers is by holding the stem of thyme at the top and running the thumb and forefinger together down the stem. The flowers can be tossed into salads, pasta and rice, or used to decorate dishes where thyme leaves have been used as a flavouring.

Because of its strong perfume, the Greeks – and later the Romans – used thyme as an incense, and also as an after-bathing fragrance. The Egyptians used it in their embalming procedures to get rid of foul smells. In the Middle Ages it was a symbol of strength and courage: ladies embroidered sprays of thyme, with a bee, on to the clothes of knights, before they went off on the Crusades. When tied in muslin it also makes an excellent bath fragrance – and is a lot cheaper than a plastic bottle full of brightly coloured bubbles!

In the kitchen, its appeal is universal; it goes with practically anything. It is, of course, essential in bouquet garnis, along with bay and parsley and it seems to work particularly well in patés and terrines (particularly hearty game or offal-based ones) or as a flavouring in meat and game stocks. Thyme is added to countless casseroles, such as oxtail, veal or hare, as it marries beautifully with onions, garlic, wine and stock. It can be added to vegetable dishes – tomatoes, courgettes, potatoes, aubergines and carrots, for example, and it makes an excellent oil, similar to rosemary oil (see page 116), which is handy for basting grilled or barbecued meats. From over a hundred varieties of thyme (such as orange or caraway), my favourite is lemon thyme (*Thymus citriodorus*), which can be used in place of garden thyme to add a unique citrus flavour. Its sweet scent is to be recommended with chicken or white fish dishes, or in desserts, such as jellies, custards and creams.

Parmesan and Thyme Soufflés

These little soufflés are delightful and so easy to make. There is no mystique about preparing or cooking soufflés. The only important thing is not to open the oven door while they are rising and to have everyone ready at table before they are even out of the oven. The flavours of the Parmesan and the thyme blend very well here, although other strong cheeses, such as mature Cheddar, will do just as well. The good thing about this recipe is that you can refrigerate the mixture to cook later – you can prepare up to 6 hours in advance, and achieve the same results – any longer and they will will not rise quite so high. (serves 6)

2 oz/50 g butter	1 heaped tablespoon thyme leaves
1½ oz/40 g plain flour	salt, pepper
½ pint/300 ml milk	3 eggs, separated plus 1 egg white
3 oz/75 g parmesan, freshly grated	

1. Preheat the oven to Gas Mark 5/190°C/375°F. Melt the butter in a pan and stir in the flour. Cook for 1 minute, stirring. Remove from the heat and gradually blend in the milk. Return to the heat and cook for a few minutes, stirring/whisking constantly, until the mixture thickens and is smooth. Remove from the heat and beat in the cheese, thyme and salt and pepper. Cool for 5 minutes then heat and stir in the egg yolks.

2. Whisk the egg whites until they are stiff. Fold a quarter into the cheese sauce. Then gently fold in the remaining egg whites.

3. Spoon the mixture into 6 buttered 3 in/8 cm ramekins. Bake in the middle of the oven for 15–18 minutes, until well-risen and golden brown on top. Serve at once.

NOTE: Do not freeze.

Carrots with Honey and Thyme

Baby vegetables are very fashionable nowadays. Some I feel are rather a waste of time; baby carrots, however, often have a better flavour than the regular-sized ones. They are usually sweeter, so the combination of baby carrots with honey and thyme is rather appropriate. Be sure the teaspoons of honey you use are level, not heaped, otherwise the carrots become too sweet. If you cannot find baby carrots, cut ordinary carrots into thick batons, before cooking. They make a delicious accompaniment to roast lamb or beef. (serves 4)

8 oz/250 g baby carrots	salt, pepper
2 level teaspoons honey	1 tablespoon thyme leaves
½ oz/15 g butter	

1. Cut the ends off the carrots and scrape them. Place in a saucepan with enough cold water to barely cover. Add the honey, butter, salt and pepper and two-thirds of the thyme leaves.

2. Bring to the boil, cover and cook for 5 minutes.

3. After 5 minutes, remove the lid, increase the heat to high and cook for a further 10 minutes, until the liquid has reduced down and become caramelised. Try not to stir; shake the pan firmly instead. Do this regularly, particularly towards the end of cooking, or they might stick.

4. Serve the carrots in a warmed dish, and sprinkle over the remaining thyme leaves.

NOTE: Do not freeze.

Aubergine and Thyme Dip

This dish is based on a couple of Middle Eastern recipe ideas. There is hummus, which is a mixture of chick peas, garlic, lemon, oil and tahini, which forms the most wonderful thick paste or dip, to be served with pitta bread. There is also the Middle Eastern combination of mint, yoghurt and vegetables, aubergine being a particular favourite. It can be deep-fried or grilled, but I shallow-fry it, then whizz it together with my other ingredients to form a thick paste, which can be served with warmed pitta bread or with crudités (slivers of raw vegetables). Thyme goes very well in this dish; I first came across the use of thyme with aubergines in Provence. There the aubergines were salted, then fried, then either layered into a gratin and baked, or made into ratatouille. Thyme, fresh from the garden, was added to both these dishes. Be sure to chop up the thyme leaves finely if it is late in the year; otherwise, try to use young, soft leaves. (makes 1 bowlful)

1 large aubergine, peeled
salt
15 oz/450 g Greek yoghurt
1 tablespoon thyme, chopped
juice of 1 orange (about 2 tablespoons)
2 tablespoons olive oil
2 garlic cloves, peeled and chopped
pepper

1. Cut the peeled aubergine into dice and lay on a plate. Sprinkle over a generous amount of salt, then leave for 20 minutes, by which time you will see the droplets of moisture forming on the aubergine.

2. Rinse them well in a colander, then pat very dry with clean tea towels.

3. Heat the oil in a frying pan and fry the aubergine cubes for about 8–10 minutes, turning often, until just soft and golden.

4. Remove and tip into a food processor with the yoghurt, thyme, orange juice and garlic. Whizz until well blended, then season with salt and pepper to taste.

5. Pour into a bowl and chill for a couple of hours, before serving with warm pitta bread or crudités. NOTE: Do not freeze.

Roast Garlic with Thyme

Eating a whole head of garlic might not sound terribly appealing to some people. But in fact, by roasting the cloves whole, without chopping, the flavour becomes sweet and smoky, without any hint of the harsh, overpowering taste of its raw state. Do not peel off the skin, only the paper-like outer casing from the head. Cut off the top, to expose the cloves, then drizzle thyme and oil over for added flavour and succulence. I like to serve this with plenty of crispy toast, like the Italian crostini, and some spreading cheese, such as a mild goat's cheese or creamy curd cheese, spread on top. It makes the most wonderful informal starter or lunch dish – only to be shared with good friends, as it is very messy! (serves 4)

4 whole heads of garlic, thin outer casing removed
2 tablespoons thyme leaves
4 tablespoons olive oil
3 oz/75 g soft goat's cheese, such as Blunt's Golden Cross,
French Chèvre or soft curd cheese
1 narrow 'ficelle' (French stick) or 4 *petits pains*, cut into thin slices

1. Preheat the oven to Gas Mark 5/190°C/375°F. With a very sharp knife, cut off the top quarter of the head of garlic, to expose the cloves. Place these on a small, oiled baking tray. Sprinkle over the thyme leaves, then the oil. Place this tray on a large baking tray and roast in the preheated oven for 20 minutes.

2. Remove from the oven and place on a board. Quickly dip the slices of bread into the oil in the small baking tray and place them on the larger baking tray. Return to the oven for a further 10 minutes, until the garlic is tender and the toasts are crispy and golden.

3. To serve, place a head of garlic with some of the thyme-flavoured oil poured over, on each plate. Offer the toasts on a platter with an accompanying dish of the soft cheese. Encourage everyone to squeeze out the garlic pulp from the cloves (as if squeezing toothpaste) and pop it on to the toast. Then top with a thin smear of the cheese. NOTE: Do not freeze.

Prawn and Asparagus Salad

The contrast of firm, succulent prawns, tender asparagus and young, soft spinach leaves is so delicious that, if you serve this as a starter, the main course will fade into insignificance in comparison. The thyme flavour comes through in a subtle yet distinctive manner; the leaves are not at all in evidence because the oil for the dressing is simply infused with the herb, then strained, before being tossed into the salad. It is the same process as making a thyme-flavoured oil, but the oil is heated here to hurry things along. Serve this accompanied by plenty of fresh crusty bread to dip into those oily juices. (serves 3–4)

4 tablespoons extra-virgin olive oil
1 heaped tablespoon thyme leaves
8 oz/250 g young spinach leaves, washed
4 oz/125 g tiger (king) prawns, cooked and peeled
salt, pepper
1 lb/500 g asparagus, trimmed
juice of 1 small lime

1. Place the oil and thyme leaves in a small saucepan and heat slowly, until it begins to bubble. Then remove from the heat, cover with a lid and leave to infuse for about 1 hour (or a minimum of 45 minutes).

2. Place the prepared spinach in a large salad bowl. Top with the prawns and season well with salt and pepper.

3. Cook the asparagus in boiling salted water for 4–5 minutes, depending on their thickness, and then drain well before adding to the spinach and prawns.

4. Strain the oil into a bowl. Add the lime juice and mix. Pour over the salad, toss well and serve at once. NOTE: Do not freeze.

Lemon Thyme Ice-cream

The fragrant taste of lemon thyme is usually associated with savoury dishes, such as chicken, fish or vegetables. It is also splendid in creamy desserts such as home-made custard or ices. Sprinkle over fresh fruit salads, particularly those made with sweet; rather than sharp fruit, as the citrus flavour accentuates the overall taste. So try with bananas, mangoes or strawberries: slice the fruit thinly, steep in some liqueur or orange juice and a little sugar, then top with a scattering of lemon thyme leaves just before serving. This ice-cream has a distinctive flavour, which I adore. It is certainly good enough to eat on its own, decorated with some lemon thyme flowers, if possible. Otherwise you can serve with hot strawberry crumble, apple pie or pear tart. (serves 4)

¼ pint/150 ml milk
½ pint/300 ml double cream
½ oz/15 g lemon thyme
4 oz/125 g caster sugar
4 large egg yolks (size 1)

1. Place the milk and cream in a saucepan with the lemon thyme. Bring slowly to the boil and then remove from the heat. Cover and allow to stand for about 30 minutes.

2. Meanwhile beat the sugar and egg yolks in a bowl over hot water until they are pale and thick; remove from the heat.

3. Strain the milk mixture into the egg mixture, beat well and tip into a heavy saucepan.

4. Cook the custard slowly, stirring constantly, until it thickens.

5. Pour into a bowl and cover tightly with clingfilm so that no skin can form. Allow to cool, then churn in an ice-cream maker, or place in a shallow freezer container in the freezer, removing to whisk every couple of hours until frozen.

Rabbit with Thyme

It was on my visit to France when I was about nineteen that I first tasted rabbit. I went into overdrive, I liked it so much. I had it cooked in red wine, white wine, with shallots, lavender and garlic; I even ate the liver in a creamy mousse. In almost all of these dishes thyme was in evidence as I was in Provence and the Pyrenees, where wild thyme is found in the hills and mountains and garden thyme grown in most gardens. This recipe seems almost too simple, yet it is so tasty. Either you can serve it at once, or – and I think it is better this way – you can leave it overnight and reheat it the next day. If you like a thicker sauce, you can reduce it down at the end, by returning to the stove and boiling, to thicken it slightly. However this also intensifies all the flavours, so take care not to over-season initially. Serve this with either boiled potatoes or – French-style – with copious amounts of crusty baguette. (serves 4)

---

1 heaped teaspoon plain flour
2 tablespoons olive oil
4–6 plump, boneless rabbit portions
4 oz/125 g smoked bacon, chopped
4 oz/125 g shallots, finely chopped
3 garlic cloves, finely chopped
2 sticks of celery, chopped
2 tablespoons thyme (stems too, unless they are very woody)
¼ pint/150 ml red wine
½ pint/300 ml dark chicken stock
salt, pepper

---

1. Preheat the oven to Gas Mark 2/150°C/300°F. Sprinkle the flour over the rabbit. Heat the oil in a heavy casserole and brown the rabbit all over. Remove with a slotted spoon and then add the bacon, shallots, garlic and celery. Fry gently for about 10 minutes.

2. Return the rabbit to the casserole and add the thyme, red wine and stock. Stir well, season with salt and pepper and bring to the boil. Remove at once, cover with a lid and place in the preheated oven for 1¾–2 hours, basting once.

3. Then, if the sauce is not as thick as you like it, remove the rabbit, keep it warm, and place the casserole over a direct heat. Boil it for 2–3 minutes, until reduced. Check and adjust your seasoning. (If you want to serve the dish on the following day, remove it from the oven after 1¼ hours, reduce the sauce if desired, then cool and refrigerate overnight. Next day, reheat for about 30 minutes at Gas Mark 4/180°C/350°F.)

4. Serve the rabbit and the sauce, piping hot.

NOTE: This dish freezes well. Defrost thoroughly and reheat at Gas Mark 4/180°C/350°F for about 45 minutes.

Roast Pheasant with Thyme

The pheasant is first roasted, then allowed to rest and is served with a beautifully creamy sauce. Thyme goes very well indeed with most game dishes, although cooking it with pheasant and venison are my favourites. It is important to keep the bird well-basted, as it can dry out very easily. By spooning over the fat, the thyme can flavour the pheasant at the same time. I serve this with either wild rice, couscous or pappardelle (pasta shaped like broad, flat ribbons), which absorb that delicious creamy sauce. (serves 2–3)

1 oz/25 g butter
1 tablespoon olive oil
1 young pheasant (about 2 lb/1 kg)
4–6 thick thyme sprigs
2 tablespoon gin
1 level tablespoon redcurrant jelly
¼ pint/150 ml double cream
salt, pepper

1. Preheat the oven to Gas Mark 6/200°C/400°F. Heat the butter and oil in a frying pan, then, once it is very hot, brown the pheasant all over. Then place it, with the fat, and the thyme, in a roasting tin and roast it in the preheated oven for about 40 minutes (allow an extra 15 minutes for a larger bird). Baste every 10 minutes.

2. Remove to a carving board and allow to rest for 10–15 minutes, covered with foil, then carve into thin slices.

3. Meanwhile, spoon off most of the fat from the roasting tin then set it directly on to the stove, over a fairly high heat. Pour in the gin and allow to bubble for a minute, then add the jelly. Stirring constantly, cook for another 1–2 minutes, until the jelly is dissolved. Then add the cream and bubble away for about 2–3 minutes, until the sauce is thick. Season with salt and pepper, then strain and serve with the pheasant.

NOTE: Do not freeze.

index